IS GOD KNOWABLE?

A Critical Study in Christian Certitudes

by

ROBERT E. ENGLAND, D. MIN.
President, Allegheny Wesleyan College

CIRCLEVILLE BIBLE COLLEGE

ISBN 0-938037-30-7
©2004

ALLEGHENY PUBLICATIONS
2161 WOODSDALE ROAD
SALEM, OH 44460

DEDICATION

To my many former students in

New Testament Greek,
Bible
and
Theology Classes

at

Salem Bible College,
Allegheny Wesleyan College,
God's Bible School & College
and
Union Bible College

Who sharpened my own thinking
as "iron sharpeneth iron"
and challenged me
to a deeper love and study of God's Word.

TABLE OF CONTENTS

INTRODUCTION

In his intriguing book *A Closer Look at Dr. Laura*, Tom Allen gives this quotation from Dr. Laura Schlessinger (whom he calls "the Queen of Talk Radio") concerning her Jewish faith: "In Jewish understanding, basically God is unknowable."[1]

As Dr. Laura sees it, God is transcendent and therefore beyond one's grasp of knowing in personal relationship. In the context of stating that God is "unknowable," Dr. Laura goes on to say, "You can struggle to study. You can struggle to understand, but ultimately, it is way beyond us. I accept that, and find peace in that."[2]

Allen commends Dr. Laura for upholding moral and biblical values. However, since she is a devout Jewess, she will define "biblical" as Old Testament, particularly the Pentateuch. As a Christian scholar, Allen defines "biblical" as both Old and New Testaments. Therefore his conclusions are sometimes different from hers on various issues.

In spite of their theological differences, Allen is convinced that Dr. Laura is on "a sincere search to know God" and therefore that "this search goes beyond the selfishness and immaturity of becoming acquainted with the Almighty in order to get more from Him." Consequently, Allen concludes that "Dr. Laura truly wants to know, love and please God."[3]

At the outset of the twenty-first century, in what has been termed the "Post-Christian Era" or even "Anti-Christian Era," how many sincere people must there be who, like Dr. Laura, think God cannot be known. However, the good news of the Bible, both Old and New Testament, is that God can be known in a personal, intimate relationship which involves a cleansing "from all sin" (I John 1:7) or "from all unrighteousness" (I John 1:9) and an impartation of God's grace so that one can "live soberly, righteously, and godly, in this present world" (Titus 2:12).

The Apostle John expresses the fundamental purpose of his Gospel rather succinctly in chapter 20, verse 31: "But these are written, that ye might *believe* that Jesus is the Christ, the Son of God; and that *believing* ye might have *life* through his name" (KJV, emphasis is mine). Thus, the Scripture is revealed as a means of precipitating faith in Christ, which in turn produces life. Obviously Jesus is speaking about spiritual life since His readers already possessed physical life.

In his First Epistle John is even more explicit as to his purpose, which is seen to take his readers a step further: "These things I have written to you that *believe* in the name of the Son of God, that you may *know* that you have *eternal life*, and that you may continue to believe in the name of the Son of God" (I John 5:13, NKJ, italics added). The "life" which John had described in his Gospel is now identified qualitatively as "eternal life." It is John's desire that believers come to "know" or be conscious of this "eternal life."

When one turns to the Gospel of Luke, it appears that the writer wants all doubt and uncertainty concerning the Gospel record to be removed from the mind of Theophilus (and all other readers as well). This is aptly stated in chapter I, verse 4: "so that you may know the certainty of the things you have been taught" (NIV). The mind of man is so constructed that it is only satisfied by the possession of a certitude of knowledge concerning the most vital questions of life.

The purpose of this study is to examine the significance and meaning of "knowledge" as found in the Gospels and the Epistles. It is readily observed that a general or natural knowledge is often expressed in the New Testament. This is the type of knowledge that all men possess by means of the physical senses, innate consciousness or mental activities. The Apostle John makes reference to this kind of knowledge in the introduction of his first epistle: "That which was from the beginning, which we have heard, which we have seen with our eyes, which we have looked at, and our hands have touched—this we proclaim concerning the Word of life" (I John I:I, NIV). The enemies of Jesus marveled at His teaching abilities and therefore asked, "How did this Man get such learning without having studied?" (John 7:15, NIV). One need not depreciate the avenues through which knowledge is obtained in a general or natural sense, for these have significance not only for a proper understanding of life from an earthly, temporal perspective, but also from a heavenly, eternal viewpoint.

The major thrust of this treatise will pertain to man's knowledge of God, although emphasis will be given to God's knowledge of man as well as man's knowledge of himself. The assertion proposed in this work may be summed up as follows: the greatest and highest knowledge available to man in this life is a knowledge of God as one's personal Savior and Lord. Nothing short of this certitude will suffice in preparing one to live a victorious Christian life or to face that unwanted enemy called death. Such knowledge is closely related to faith, not only a faith that believes in God's existence, but one which also believes that "He is a rewarder of them that diligently seek Him" (KJV). Furthermore, knowledge is also related to truth, which is identified with that which actually exists. Perhaps the best single word to describe truth is "reality." Truth is both actual and factual. To believe an untruth does not lead to knowledge, at least not in the normal usage of the term, unless one refers to a knowledge of unreality. On the other hand, to believe truth does lead to the possession of knowledge. Hence, Jesus promised, "You shall know the truth and the truth shall make you free" (John 8:32, NKJ). In light of New Testament data this thesis will also propose that the most real of all realities is a personal, intimate knowledge of a right relationship with God.

This study will be approached from a holistic viewpoint. Since man is tri-partite, it is to be expected that body, mind and spirit will interact with each other in the acquisition of knowledge. When one facet of truth is unduly stressed at the expense of other equally important aspects, serious problems are created. Therefore, it is necessary to maintain a proper balance. One must be cautious about the options laid forth by scholars who say it is an "either. . .or" proposition. In many cases it is safer to acknowledge a "both. . .and" possibility.

In Part One it will be necessary to give some attention to the concepts of knowledge which were held in the world during the first century A.D. These, of course, had their roots in the centuries preceding Christ's Advent. Only against the backdrop of this preparatory period can one appreciate the significance of the New Testament revelation.

The world of the New Testament had been Hellenized. Therefore, a brief sketch of the history of Greece is set forth in order to lay a foundation for the unfolding contributions which the Greeks made to the world into which the New Testament came. The retrospect of history provides a renewed appreciation for the providential acts of Jehovah.

A discussion of the two major divisions of the ancient world, namely the Orient and the Occident, follows. Particular distinctions and emphases of the peoples in each geographical and cultural setting will be seen to have made its mark upon the pre-Christian world. Intuitive and subjective elements tend to characterize the Oriental while methodical, rational and objective qualities tend to describe the Occidental.

Furthermore, it is of special import to observe the ways by which men sought to come to a knowledge of God. In the sixth and fifth centuries before Christ the Greeks were persuaded that they could attain to a knowledge of God by mere intellectual processes.

Not only was the intellect said to be a means of knowing God; another teaching declared that God was to be known by emotional experiences. Such emphasis was especially seen in the so-called Mystery Religions. These were apparently developed as a result of blending Western religions with Eastern mysticism. Passion plays were produced, based upon the story of some god who suffered greatly, died and was then resurrected. The various activities relating to the viewers and the actors were intended to produce an emotional experience where one could "feel" God. How fleeting was such an experience. Although the Mystery Religions proclaimed salvation and immortality, they did not satisfy the deepest longings of man's soul.

The most important contribution to the world of the New Testament was Judaism out of which Christianity sprang. The key element in the matter of knowing God is not intellect or emotion, but obedience to God's commandments. Therefore the right response for man is not a reasoning process, but rather a submission to the will of God. In such a submission man's will is activated to do the will of God; this results in a revelation which produces knowledge of a right relationship with Jehovah. A lack of knowledge is traced to disobedience, as seen in Hosea 4:1ff. Of course, God can only be known insofar as He has chosen to reveal Himself. A reverential fear of God is the starting point for man if he would attain a personal knowledge of the Lord (Proverbs 1:7; 2:1-6).

Part Two is devoted to an examination of the most important Greek words for *know* and *knowledge*. However, it is not necessary for the reader to have studied New Testament Greek to gain helpful insights from this part of the study. The Greek words are often transliterated into English spellings so that one who has not studied Greek can at least pronounce the words with some degree of fluency, however different that may be from that of a polished scholar.

One may decided to omit Part Two and simply pass on to Part Three and then return to the word study later. The content of Part Two is such that some readers will need to go over the materials two or three times to reap the greatest benefit.

In dealing with each Greek term a consistent pattern is followed in the examination made. Each word is traced historically to note its meanings and applications in Classical, Hellenistic, and Septuagint usages. The most intensive and extensive treatment is given to the most oft-used verbs, namely γινώσκω (ginosko) and οἶδα (oida). Other verbs discussed are ἐπιγινώσκω (epiginosko), ἐπίσταμαι (epistamai), and συνίημι (suniemi). The two nouns, γνῶσις (gnosis) and ἐπίγνωσις (epignosis) are also examined. Then a section dealing with both similarities and contrasts follows. Special interest centers upon the New Testament usage. Scholars have long debated the question, "Do classical distinctions hold true in New Testament literature?" Assessments are made and conclusions are drawn within and at the close of this section.

Part Three focuses attention upon various aspects of knowledge in the New Testament. Particularly during the twentieth century, scholars have discussed, debated and written numerous works on the phenomenon known as Gnosticism. With the translation of Gnostic literature found near Nag Hammadi new light has been shed forth. A controversial issue has centered on the matter of an alleged pre-Christian Gnosticism. Was there such a phenomenon as pre-Christian Gnosticism, or was there only a non-Christian type of Gnosticism in existence before the emergence of Christianity? Did Christianity borrow terminology from Gnostic systems, or was it a matter of Gnosticism borrowing from Christianity? Were some of the enemies of true Christianity against whom John and Paul wrote Gnostics? If so, was it a full-fledged Gnosticism or was it simply an elementary stage? These are valid questions which demand the attention and intellectual honesty of the New Testament scholar. German writers in the past century have usually chosen a pre-Christian Gnosticism. The weakness in their conclusions is seen to be a lack of evidence from early literary sources. Gnostic literature is generally dated from the second century A.D. onward. Consequently, much of the reconstruction work of a pre-Christian Gnosticism is based upon the uncertain foundation of a priori assumptions that are definitely less than "assured evidence." It does appear that Gnostic systems were at least in an incipient form by the time the latter New Testament books were written. Many of the British and American scholars have tended to hold to this position.

The major emphasis in the latter section of Part Three is directed toward the means whereby man comes to know God. Perhaps the most far-reaching manner in which God discloses Himself is by means of His created universe. This natural means of revelation is extended to all of mankind and becomes a criterion of judgment for those who have never had the privilege of possessing a Bible. God can hold all men accountable because His creation testifies to the fact of His power and His divinity, as stated in Romans, chapter one.

Not only has God manifested Himself in a general revelation, He has more intimately made Himself known through His written Word, the sacred Scriptures. This objective record has been inspired by God Himself. It reveals qualities and characteristics of God which nature can never disclose.

The knowledge of God is further unveiled through the Person of Christ. In Him is to be seen the fullest and the most perfect revelation of God. Christ is the "express image" of the Father, and the one who has seen the Son has also seen the Father, according to the Gospel of John, chapter fourteen and verse nine. The knowledge of God is mediated through Christ, for "no one knows the Father except the Son and those to whom the Son chooses to reveal Him" (Matthew 11:27, NIV). Christ came to earth to provide redemption that He might effect a reconciliation between God and man so that lost mankind might come to know God as Savior and Lord.

One final means of knowing God demands attention, namely that of the Holy Spirit. Christ came to provide redemption and reveal the Father; the Holy Spirit came to apply redemption and to disclose the Son. John has expressed the knowledge of salvation communicated by the Holy Spirit thus: "We know that we live in Him and He in us, because He has given us of His Spirit" (I John 4:13, NIV).

What greater goal can one have than that of the Apostle Paul as expressed in Philippians 3:10, 11, "I want to know Christ and the power of His resurrection and the fellowship of sharing in His sufferings, becoming like Him in His death, and so, somehow, to attain to the resurrection from the dead" (NIV).

PART I

PRE-CHRISTIAN PREPARATORY PERIOD

The Apostle Paul declared that Jesus came into the world "when the fullness of the time was come" (Galatians 4:4). Such a declaration presupposes that there must have been a period of preparation preceding and paving way for "the fullness of the time" to finally arrive. The New Testament is rooted in and structured upon the Old Testament. If any single term describes the entire scope of the Old Economy it is the word "preparation." However, God's purposes in Christ were not limited to the Jews only but were to encompass the whole world. It is therefore to be expected that the entire ancient world would be involved in this pre-Christian period of preparation.

Jesus was born into a world which was under the political control of the Roman Empire. It is more precise, however, to call the world of the first century A.D. the "Greco-Roman world." Indeed, the Romans were so impressed and captivated by Grecian contributions to the ancient world that they did not try to remove them. One can hardly overstate the importance of Greek influence upon the world into which the New Testament came.

The purpose of Part I is to lay a foundation for the study of "knowledge" in the New Testament. Special attention will be given to man's knowledge of God. Therefore, it is necessary to survey the centuries prior to Christ's advent in order to see what place of importance was given to this subject. By means of this background one will be able to appreciate more fully the message of the New Testament on this vital theme.

The major thrust of this study will treat the most important type of knowledge attainable by man, namely, knowledge of God. The faculty of knowledge in man is directly linked to the image of God in which Adam was created. In his unfallen state man possessed knowledge in both the intellectual and the moral realms. With the fall of the first man and woman the moral image was utterly shattered. Although the intellectual aspects were marred, they remained intact, for without such powers man could not be man. The depth of moral depravity is vividly portrayed in Psalm 14:2, which declares that God looked upon mankind to determine whether "there were any who did understand and seek God." In the next verse He reports His discovery: "They are *all* gone aside, they are *all* together become filthy: there is *none* that doeth good, no, *not one*" (emphasis is mine). Verse four raises this pertinent question: "Have all the workers of iniquity no knowledge?" In light of Biblical data does not this question demand a resounding NO? On the positive side, provision has been made through Christ for the restoration of this moral aspect of knowledge. Paul reveals that in the new birth one puts on the "new self, which is being renewed in *knowledge* in the image of its Creator" (Colossians 3:10).

As one examines the pre-Christian era it is imperative that a proper perspective be maintained concerning heathen peoples who did not possess the written prepositional Word of God, the Scriptures. The Apostle John asserts that Jesus was "the true Light, which lighteth every man that cometh into the world" (John 1:9). In some sense, therefore, all men are illumined through their consciences regarding moral knowledge. This fact is reinforced by Romans 1:19, "what may be known about God is plain to them" (NIV). In verse 20 Paul explains how God has made it known: "For since the creation of the world God's invisible qualities—his eternal power and divine nature—have been clearly seen, being understood from what has been made, so that men are without excuse" (NIV). It is evident that God has not left pagan peoples without the inner witness of conscience and the outer witness of creation which point back to a Creator to whom man is responsible. While these witnesses do not reveal the plan of salvation, they do indicate why men of all times and places have a religious capacity which seeks to know and worship God or a god.

Chapter One

HISTORICAL SURVEY OF GREECE

Since this chapter will devote much space to a discussion of contributions made by the Greeks in the centuries prior to the Advent of Christ, it does seem necessary to sketch a brief history of Greece in order to better understand subsequent topics. This section will be treated under a six-fold division.

Early Period

According to Peter Arnott the history of Greece actually begins on the Island of Crete.[4] The Cretan or Minoan Empire enjoyed its fullest bloom from about 3000-1400 B.C. The finds of archaeologists reveal an elegant and luxurious civilization.

M. I. Finley claims that the first migration southward into what is now known as the Greek peninsula took place among people who spoke Greek approximately 2000 B.C., at least prior to 1900 B.C.[5] Finley Hooper declares that the Greek-speaking peoples from the north began moving southward into the Balkan peninsula about 2600 B.C. but did not journey into the most southern portions until about 1900.[6] No doubt both men are correct, but apparently what Finley is calling the first migration southward is actually the second major movement of people from their earlier home in Europe.

About 1400 B.C. various Minoan cities were destroyed, but the means of destruction is not known. One suggestion is that the conquerors came from the mainland to the north and were the first genuine Greeks. Yet another theory points to destruction by natural causes brought forth by an earthquake. Whatever the exact cause may have been, it does appear that the destructive work of decay had been operative for some time. Arnott describes the step-by-step developments as follows:

This rich and ultimately decadent civilization, so secure in its prosperity that its cities were built without walls, had already yielded to the influence of a new power emerging from the North. Successive waves of migrants had moved down into Greece and established cities there. These were the people we call Indo-Europeans. There [sic] origins are still much disputed, though it is clear that they came of different racial stock from the earlier inhabitants of the Mediterranean. They spoke of a language which was the parent of Greek, Latin, Sanskrit, Celtic and so ultimately of English, German and the Romance languages. None of this language was written down—we are talking here of a preliterary society—but it can, by a quasi-algebraic process, be reconstructed at least in outline from its known offspring. The people also brought new deities, and new customs.

Thus mainland Greece, which had earlier been probed by Cretan colonizers, fell under this new influence. The immigrants built strong cities; their language developed into what we now know as Greek, and they eventually began to write this language down.[7]

Mycenaean Period

This innovative period ranged from about 1400-1200 B.C. and is identified as the "technically advanced Bronze-Age civilization."[8] A glance at a map of ancient Greece reveals that Mycenae was located approximately twenty miles southwest of Corinth.

Mycenae was situated upon a rugged, fortified hill which overlooked the rich, fertile plain of Argos. Articles uncovered in burial shafts seem to reflect an influence from Crete.[9]

With the fall of Mycenae other cities began to amass power and yet were independent of one another. The most important of these were Athens, Corinth, Thebes and Sparta.

Dark Age

Following the Bronze Age is a period of about four centuries that is sometimes called the Greek "Dark Age" because so little is known about it. Yet it is not correct to think of this era as one complete retrogression, for, as Finley notes, it was the time of the discovery of iron and the birth of the "Greek Society" which precipitated "the new world, the historical Greek world," a world which he claims "was altogether different, economically, politically and culturally."[10] Sometime after the Trojan War the conquering Achaeans were themselves conquered, apparently by vast numbers of tribesmen from the north. In endeavoring to relate this invasion with both earlier and later events Hooper offers the following possible reconstruction:

> Sometime in the past beyond recall, the ancestors of all these Greek-speaking peoples had lived together somewhere in the Danubian region of central Europe. For reasons we know nothing about, the various groups became separated and in the course of time they were even speaking different dialects. Moreover, because of their separate experiences and contacts, they eventually lived on vastly different cultural levels. The first Greek-speaking peoples who moved south came under the influence of the older Cretan and Egyptian civilizations and built impressive Mycenaean civilization, but about the twelfth century B.C. their flourishing centers were put to the torch by other Greek-speaking peoples who, far from appreciating what they found, did not save it for themselves.
>
> The arrival of these rude relations has generally been treated as a single event and called the Dorian invasion. This was because those who spoke the Dorian dialect comprised the largest segment of the invaders and spread themselves over the widest area of the Aegean world. . . .
>
> At the same time the Dorians were arriving, other tribes were making inroads from the north. They spoke a dialect which, though closely related to the Dorian, was distinctly different. While the Dorians were living in Macedonia these people were settled nearby to the west, in southern Epirus. From there some of them moved due south across the Corinthian Gulf and into Elis, the northwestern section of the Peloponnesus. Others, the Thessaloi and the Boiotoi moved east and southeast and gave their names to the lands where they finally settled.[11]

It does appear that most of the inhabitants who fled from the Dorian invaders crossed the Aegean Sea and settled in the coastal areas of

Asia Minor. The district of Ionia developed into a progressive cultural center that was tailored for intellectual pursuits. Especially influential was the city of Miletus from which the first philosophers were to emerge.

The Dark Age was not totally void of literature and art. The most famous epic poems, *The Iliad* and *The Odyssey* by Homer, were probably penned toward the close of this period. It may be that Hesiod's writings fit into this same time frame, although another suggestion would date them into the late eighth or early seventh centuries.[12] The pottery of this era made use of a variety of geometric patterns.

Hooper observes that the Dark Age of Greece, like that of Europe after the fall of Rome, was characterized by "depression, illiteracy, and disorganization," and yet he wisely adds that both of these periods closed with the ushering in of a "revival of trade and town life,..."[13]

Archaic Period

This historical segment covers approximately three centuries, from about 800 or 750-500 B.C.[14] It was indeed a period of progress, yet the very nature of the varied city-states demanded distinctions.

The monarchical reigns of the Dark Age gave way to a new oligarchical system in which authority was vested in an aristocracy which was composed of certain families. It is not known how this transition took place, but once it did, the aristocrats had control of all, or nearly all, the land which they ruled "partly through formal institutions, councils and magistracies; partly by marital and kinship connexions as an Establishment; partly by the intangible authority which came from their ancestry, for they could all produce genealogies taking them back to famous 'heroes' (and from there, often enough, to one of the gods)."[15]

As one would expect, conflicts developed between the rulers and the ruled. One of the problems that developed pertained to the growth of the populace. Since neither the mainland nor the islands of Greece can support a large population, it became necessary to seek new dwelling places by the middle of the eighth century. This "Colonization" movement, which lasted for about two centuries, tended to dissipate some of the friction between the oligarchy and the people.

There were two major pursuits in the placement of surplus peoples. The first movement began about 740 and extended westward, to the islands as well as the coast of the Ionian Sea, then to Sicily and the southern portions of Italy, and later on (latter part of the seventh century) to southern France as well as Libya. The second migration began about 650 and mainly moved east and northeast. The Black Sea was practically surrounded by these Greek migrants.

These communities were not "colonies" in the usual understanding of the term, but were actually independent units that were not even bound to their "mother-city" from whence they sprang. It is thought that these communities numbered as high as 1500 by the close of the migrations.

The migration movement was not a cure-all for the problem back home. In fact, the factions among the aristocrats themselves helped to precipitate a new Greek institution, namely the "tyrant." Although it was supported by the military, it did not originally bear an unpleasant connotation; it simply meant that the one who had gained control of the government did not have a legally constituted authority. It is true that military might was often abused in the process of time and therefore became a curse.

Also emerging in this period, particularly in the sixth century, was the figure of a lawgiver. Of special interest was the situation at Athens. In 594 Solon was chosen by the Athenians to be their lawgiver and was given the responsibility of bringing reform to the state. Solon endeavored to exalt justice, to insure that neither aristocrats nor common people would be treated unjustly. Although he was unable to alleviate Athens' economical problems, a step in the right direction had been taken.

Within a generation the reign of the Athenian tyrant Peisistratus began, ranging from about 745-727. Although he was in fact a noble, it was during his reign that a compromise was effected with the peasants concerning land use and finance. Best of all, the political power structure of the aristocrats was now broken. Thus, one can readily see that the reign of the tyrant was, in effect, a transition step between the aristocracy and the city-state of the Classical Period.

Classical Period

This period covers the fifth and most of the fourth centuries. It is in many respects the most glorious period in the entire history of Greece. Athens had progressed to the political realm of a democracy. If any one person is to be esteemed for bringing Athens into a democratic system, it is a man from the Alcmeonidae family by the name of Cleisthenes. Under his leadership and reforms the city-state of Athens burst forth into a freedom it had probably never before experienced.

When the fifth century opened, Aristagoras of Miletus led Greek colonists in a revolt against the mighty power of Persia. Some time later vengeance was meted out and Miletus, that great cultural center of Ionia, was utterly destroyed. When the Persians came to the mainland of Greece, they were surprisingly defeated by a smaller army of Athenians who had not been able to secure the aid of the Spartans. With the destruction of Miletus the new center of learning and culture was destined to be Athens. Arnott sums up the importance of Athens as follows:

> Throughout the fifth century Athens' swift rise to power gave her not only political but cultural supremacy, so that when in this period we speak of Greek art, drama, sculpture, it is nearly always Athenian that we mean; most of the enduring products of Greek civilization have come from Athens in the fifth century B.C.[16]

Some of the most outstanding philosophers, scholars, and writers lived during this "Golden Age." More will be said about this period in a later chapter.

The military victories of Athens over Persia effected a cohesion among Greek states which would not have otherwise been reached. As a result of those victories Athens replaced Sparta as the military hero. After a long period of struggles Athens and Sparta were ready to declare a fifty-year peace, thereby stopping competition one with another.

With the loss of several allied states Athens fell from her pinnacle of power in 404. Never to regain the power held in the fifth century, she nevertheless continued for the next several centuries as "the recognized fountainhead of learning, of art, of philosophy."[17]

Hellentistic Period

The Hellenistic era begins with Alexander the Great. The term "Hellenistic" was coined to denote the Greek culture after Alexander in distinction to the Greek culture prior to him which is called "Hellenic." Hans Jonas declares that the term "Hellenistic" was introduced "to denote not just the enlargement of the polis culture to a cosmopolitan culture and the transformations inherent in the process alone but also the change of character following from the reception of oriental influences into this enlarged whole."[18]

In the latter half of the fourth century Alexander's father, King Philip of Macedon, began moving southward, overcoming one after another of the city-states until he conquered all except Sparta. Following the assassination of Philip about 336, Alexander picked up the reins. With the strength of Greece behind him Alexander took the offensive and moved eastward winning battle after battle until he had possessed the entire Persian Empire. Alexander took the Greek culture into much of the known world and then died prematurely in 323 B.C. Although Alexander's kingdom was divided and later displaced in the first century B.C., the Greek culture had made an indelible imprint upon the world into which the New Testament would soon come. Alexander at least prepared the world linguistically for the coming of the Messiah and the New Testament.

Chapter Two

THE EAST AND THE WEST

As one surveys the ancient world it soon becomes evident that there were two major divisions, both geographically and culturally, namely the East and the West. In this chapter attention will be focused upon the distinctions between the peoples of the East and the West, especially as they relate to intellectual activities.

Geographical Factors

Do geographical factors affect the attitudes and activities of a people? Does the density of population have any bearing on the lifestyle of a particular community or nation?

Scholars may differ in regard to details, but there appears to be a general consensus that the above elements do play an influential part in the formation of one's pattern of living.

The East. By this term reference is made to Egypt and those lands which are east of ancient Greece. Egypt had once been a mighty empire but had been displaced by Assyria who was the mistress of the ancient world for a long time during which the northern Kingdom of Israel was carried into captivity in the latter part of the eighth century. In a three-way contest between Egypt, Babylon and Assyria, Babylon emerged as the victor in the closing part of the seventh century. This reign of supremacy was short-lived, however, and came to an abrupt end when Persia toppled Babylon. Thus, for many centuries in the ancient world political and military power were held by peoples of the East.

A glance at a map reveals that as one moves from Egypt in a northeasterly direction to Assyria, Babylon and Persia most of the land is barren, useless desert except for "the Fertile Crescent." These factors meant that the people must confine their dwelling places to areas near the waterways.

Believing that geography had an effect upon Egyptians, Edith Hamilton describes Egypt as "a fertile valley of rich river soil, low-lying, warm, monotonous, a slow-flowing river, and beyond, the limitless desert," and therefore she concludes that Egypt "submitted and suffered and turned her face toward death."[19]

The West. By this term is meant Greece and those nations to the West. Although people of the East were the powers over much of the known world prior to the advent of Christ, it is of interest to note that the mantle fell to people of the West in the last four and a quarter centuries before Christ. The major interest in this study is concerned with Greece.

Finley Hooper draws a contrast between Greece, which only had about 50,000 square miles of land surface in both the mainland and the islands, with the state of Kansas which has approximately 82,000 square miles.[20] A further contrast is significant; while only a portion of the mountainous terrain of Greece is usable, most of the flatlands of Kansas are productive farm soil.

Once again a map is helpful. One will observe that Greece is surrounded by water except to the north. Only the narrow isthmus connected the southern peninsula known as the Peloponnesus with the northern mainland of Greece. A map reveals that no part of Greece was very many miles from a large body of water. Such a setting was bound to produce a seafaring people.

C. M. Bowra correctly asserts that the geographical elements in Greece have had "a primary influence in shaping the destiny of its people."[21] He further adds:

> Such a land demands that its inhabitants should be tough, active, entertaining, and intelligent. . . . Geographical circumstances formed the Geek character by forcing it to make the most of its natural aptitudes in a hard struggle with the earth and the elements.[22]

Another development which took place because of the lay of land was that of little, independent communities which settled into the small valleys and plains that were often surrounded by mountains. This meant that one community would often be entirely isolated from another community that would be situated only a short distance away. Arnott explains the development of these communities as follows:

> As new waves of immigrants moved in from the north, they settled in these valleys; often, one wave would not intermingle with another but pass by it, kept off by the barrier mountains. Thus the country developed as a collection of separate and distinct small settlements, with different origins, different customs, constitutions, religions and ways of life. It is false to speak of Greek history as though it were the history of a nation. It was no such thing. Rather, it was the history of an agglomeration of small and quarrelsome political entities, first one and then another predominating. This was not entirely a matter of geography; the small-settlement pattern was acceptable to the Greek temperament for other reasons, but geography created the mould wherein such a pattern might be shaped.[23]

In her description of Greece Miss Hamilton says it is "a country of sparse fertility and keen, cold winter, all hills and mountains sharp cut in stone, where strong men must work hard to get their bread," but then she declares that in contrast to Egypt, Greece "resisted and rejoiced and turned full-face to life."[24]

Although geographical factors do not paint a full picture of the development of any civilization, one must conclude, however, that they do play a vital part that cannot be omitted from any meaningful discussion of the subject.

Mind and Spirit

Even a cursory examination of the characteristics of the Orient and the Occident reveal clear distinctions in the ways each come to a point of knowledge. Generally speaking, the East has tended to give greatest emphasis to man's spirit, while the West has usually given stress to man's intellectual processes.

The East. In the Orient it is generally conceded that man comes to a possession of knowledge or an apprehension of truth, not by analysis or step-by-step mental processes, but by an "intuitive leap." Knowledge especially involves man's spirit, for if he is to know anything there must be a personal experience—his emotions, his feeling capacity must be activated.

F.S.C. Northrop elaborates upon this aspect of Oriental knowledge and also draws fundamental contrasts with the Occident:

> For the genius of the East is that it has discovered a type of knowledge and has concentrated its attention continuously, as the West has not, upon a portion of the nature of things which can be known only by being experienced. The West, to be sure, begins with experience in the gaining of its type of knowledge and returns to experimentally controlled portions of experience in the confirmation of that knowledge. But the Western type of knowledge tends to be formally and doctrinally expressed in logistically developed, scientific and philosophical treatises. The syntactically constructed sentences of these treatises, by the very manner in which they relate the key factors in their subject matter, enable the reader, with but incidental references to items of his imagination or bits of his experience, to comprehend what is designated. Consequently, in the West, although appeals to experience are necessarily present and continuously made by the scientific, philosophic and theological experts who verify and construct its doctrine, nevertheless, providing the reader has an elementary acquaintance with the rules of grammar, and masters the Western technique for understanding things in terms of their verbally designated relations to each other, it is not necessary for the Western reader to squat upon his haunches, like a sage in an Indian forest, immediately apprehending and contemplating what is designated. Being concerned, as the West tends continuously to be, with the factor in the nature of things which is not immediately apprehended, but is instead merely suggested as a possible hypothesis by the immediately apprehended items of his own direct experience, is enabled to a great extent by his books and texts alone to gain the type of knowledge which the West values, and to know the factor in the nature of things which this Western type of knowledge designates.[25]

The ancient Oriental world was particularly engrossed in the spirit realm, the invisible world.[26] This fact is clearly seen in the lives of the Egyptians. For multiplied centuries they seemed to give less attention to life than to death, for their art continuously expresses the latter. Two reasons may be cited for bringing about such a morbid state in Egypt. First of all were the wretched conditions and the sufferings to which the masses were subjected. The extensive and difficult building of massive monuments was costly in terms of human lives. Even those in higher circles could not be certain of security, for the lives of all seemed to hang in the balances of the monarch. Under such circumstances one can readily see why men lost hope of ever attaining to a happy life in this world; therefore, they looked forward to death through which they might attain peace and comfort. These suffering peoples were not challenged to use their minds, for those in misery do not usually seek help by means of the intellect.

A second reason for the state of affairs in Egypt was rooted in the priesthood. The priests soon learned that their power leverage was weakened if they taught the people to think for themselves. Consequently, it was decided that the populace must be kept in ignorance so that they would be dependent upon the priesthood.

Hamilton sums up the ancient scene in the following manner: "The misery of the people was the opportunity of the priest. Not only an ignorant populace but one subjugated and wretched was their guarantee. With men's thought directed more and more toward the unseen world, and with the keys to it firmly in their own grasp, their terrific power was assured."[27]

In India the cleavage between mind and spirit was even greater. Reality is not related to the temporal or the tangible; only spirit is said to be real. The material universe is only an illusion. Hamilton correctly unfolds the reason so many Indians have given undue attention to the spirit:

> This is always man's way out when the facts of life are too bitter and too black to be borne. When conditions are such that life offers no earthly hope, somewhere, somehow, men must find a refuge. Then they fly from the terror without to the

citadel within, which famine and pestilence and fire and sword cannot shake.[28]

The West. In contrast to the Orient the Occident tends to give proper emphasis to the mind. One comes to know by observation, analysis, and logical thought processes so that one may find causes for effects. Northrop states it this way:

> Confronted with himself and nature, Western man arrives by observation and scientific hypothesis at a theoretical conception of the character of these two factors. This theoretical conception even when determined by empirically and experimentally controlled scientific methods, always affirms more, as Democritus and Plato were the first to see, than bare facts by themselves provide.[29]

It is refreshing indeed to note the emergence of a living, vibrant civilization in Greece which arose out of the ancient world that had come to give an undue emphasis to spirit at the expense of mind. Out of the Dark Age sprang forth a new kind of Greek world which was inspired by its past history to espouse the challenge for heroism in both body and mind.[30]

Pythagoras developed a three-fold classification for mankind, the first of which is most important: (1) those who search after knowledge; (2) those who aspire for honor; and (3) those who strive for personal gain.[31]

Werner Jaeger sees this new intellectual breakthrough of the Greeks as "a fundamental advance on the great peoples of the Orient, a new stage in the development of society," which he contrasts with Egyptian history that is characterized as "a dreadful rigidity which is almost fossilization."[32]

Students of Greek history have often said that these innovative Greeks were not under the oppressive hand of superstition but were the first people whose minds were not held in bondage. R. F. Earp takes issue with those who make simplistic statements without further explanation.[33] He admits that the Greeks were not under the pressure of a priestly system, nor were most of them fearful of unfair treatment by the gods; nevertheless, there is much evidence of superstition in one form or another as well as a fear of offending a god or gods.[34] With this basic conclusion Hooper agrees and further states that the romantic stress of some writers has given the "impression that the Greeks sought rational solutions and were imaginative and intellectually curious as a people."[35] Opposing such a broad viewpoint, Hooper declares that the largest part of the populace always sought security in the realms of magic and superstition, but he does admit that enough Greeks sought rational answers "so as to enable a whole people to be associated with the beginnings of philosophy including the objectivity of scientific inquiry."[36]

The warning of Hooper and Earp is in order. Care must be taken in drawing conclusions. One must avoid making broad generalizations without qualifying such statements so that he does not misrepresent the facts.

Another scholar who feels some writers have failed to strike a proper balance is Edwyn Bevan, who thinks that too much has been made of distinctions between the Oriental and the Occidental: ". . . there is no faculty possessed by any race of men but is possessed in some measure by all; the difference is one of proportion. The most primitive savage exercises reason in his own degree."[37]

On the other hand, Bevan suggests that the best way to express the western type of culture is by the terminology of "Rationalistic Civilization."[38] However, he says that some discussions have not been factual and gives the following example: if one claims that Orientals have no love for nature, such as flowers, by citing examples from India, let him journey on eastward and he will find that the Japanese have a greater love for nature in the realms of flowers than many Occidentals do.[39]

Without question Bevan has made a valid point. There are many parts which make up the whole. The weight of evidence does point to the dawning of a new spirit in Greece at the beginning of the sixth century. Bowra has expressed it well:

> There was a desire to understand things more exactly, to penetrate the mystery which enveloped them, to explain them

in rational language, and to find principles and rules in nature rather than the inexplicable whims which myth ascribed to the gods.[40]

Although the Greeks gave intellectual pursuits a place of priority, it would be entirely erroneous to conclude that this was their only interest. With the Greeks it was not a matter of mind *or* spirit, but it was mind *and* spirit. One was not seen to be incompatible with the other. The importance of man's spirit is seen in the poetry, art, and religion of the Greeks. Hamilton correctly concludes that "in Greece the mind and the spirit met on equal terms."[41]

It is also important to note that the Greeks paid special attention to physical, bodily activities. Greek literature and art reveal that they gave themselves to all kinds of games and athletic contests. In Plato's *Timaeus* an elderly priest expressed himself to Solon thus: "O Solon, Solon, you Greeks are always children: there is not such a thing as an old Greek . . . . You are young in soul, every one of you."[42] In contrast to this, such an emphasis on play and games is noticeably absent among Egyptians and Mesopotamians.[43]

By way of summary, one may say that the peoples of the East in the ancient world were limited to and bound by an undue stress and an over-emphasis on man's spirit. By contrast, the Greeks, from a far healthier perspective, gave due recognition to body, mind, and spirit.

The Arts

Before concluding the discussion of distinctions between the Orientals and the Occidentals, brief attention should be given to the arts, which always reveal a great deal about any people.

The East. One would naturally expect to find clear-cut differences in the realm of the arts in light of the above distinctions already discussed. It is especially interesting to discover that both the geographical factors and mind and/or spirit played a vital role in the development of the arts.

In Egypt, for example, the geographical situation forced the populace to dwell on the narrow strip of land on either side of the Nile. Because of this fact, the political realm was under the centralized control of one man, the Pharaoh, who, according to Hooper, "dominated every area of thought and action."[44] Under such a political regime one could not expect writers or artists to express individuality in their productions. Furthermore, as noted earlier, the Egyptians were under the power of the priesthood which meant that imposed shackles would greatly limit the type of literature and art that would be accepted by both government and religion.

One of the clearest expressions about this stereotyped fossilization of the arts in Egypt is expressed by the Athenian stranger in Plato's *Laws*:

> It appears that long ago they determined on the rule of which we are now speaking, that the youth of a State should practice in their rehearsals postures and tunes that are good: these they prescribed in detail and posted up in the temples, and outside this official list it was, and still is, forbidden to painters and all other producers of postures and representations to introduce any innovation or invention, whether in such productions or in any other branch of music, over and above the traditional forms. And if you look there, you will find that the things depicted or graven there 10,000 years ago (I mean what I say, not loosely but literally 10,000) are no whit better or worse than the productions of to-day, but wrought with the same art."[45]

In India one was not hampered by political restraints but the religious die was cast with such a strong emphasis on one's spirit which, of course, allowed much freedom of expression in regard to one's own visions and personal experiences. The fact that the material, visible world was considered to be illusory added to the probability that Indian art would be of a wide variety. It is not strange, therefore, that the art of the Indians is often so grotesque, so different from the normal patterns exhibited in this here-and-now world.

Edith Hamilton states that the Oriental artists who despised this visible, material world had to make use of symbolism and yet possessed much liberty in the entire process:

> The mystical artist is free to make use of reality and to dispense with it as he pleases. He is at liberty also to improvise his own symbolism which can be of the simplest: many arms to express multiform power; many breasts to show spiritual nourishment; a sublimated pictorial writing. His only restraint comes from within his own self, but, despising as he does the outside world, predisposed against seeing real things as beautiful, the artist within him, who must find spiritual significance somewhere, is irresistibly impelled toward the pattern which he can make symbolic, and so, significant.[46]

Indeed there is something about the art of the Indians that suggests a broad gulf of separation between the rational mind and the emotional spirit of man. In searching for reality it is ironic that so much emphasis is laid upon the transient, subjective nature of finite man.

The West. The very factors that affected Egypt, namely the geographical and the religious, also affected Greece, but in opposite ways. As mentioned earlier, the rugged mountain terrain produced numerous communities which were independent of one another. Unity was not a strong characteristic of the Greeks. In fact, history indicates that there were very few times when the ancient Greeks were fused together as a united people. As a result, the Greek writer, painter, or sculptor was not generally placed under the limitations of a political yoke. Hooper declares that if a poet were forced to leave a city on the orders of a ruling tyrant he could always find a friendly city ruled by aristocrats that would offer him a haven; therefore, "Greece offered the artist and the thinker the possibility of becoming a free agent, if he were willing to travel."[47]

Likewise, in the religious realm the differences were great. The Greeks were not under the dominion of an oppressive priesthood. Consequently, the Greek writers and artists had the freedom to express themselves in new and varied ways, unlike the Egyptians.

While the Oriental artist often went off to an isolated place to meditate and produce a finished work, the Greek depended upon the visible, tangible world of persons, places, and things to provide him the needed materials for his work. There was absolutely no need for him to separate his intellect from his spirit—the two should function together.

In contrast to the Oriental patterns which are not replicas of what we know in this world, the Greek artists portrayed that which is true to life. Sometimes they were too plain; it is unfortunate that various paintings and statues depicted man and woman or god and goddess in the nude. Hamilton points out that even the Olympic god Hermes is depicted as "a perfectly beautiful human being, no more, no less;" for the only identifying mark of his divinity was his "beauty."[48] Greek art was simple, plain, lifelike, not cluttered with excessive ornament as were the Indian works.

The same characteristics mark the literature of the Greeks. The oldest and in many respects the most important kind of literature in ancient times was that of poetry. Bowra says that the Greeks had distinct words to identify the different kinds of poetry, but if they wanted to refer to all of them together, they used the term "sophia" which literally means "wisdom" but can also denote "skill."[49]

No one can properly deny the fact that the Greeks united both mind and spirit along with political freedom to stimulate creativity in the visual and written arts. Truly the lines of demarcation were clearly drawn between the Oriental and the Occidental.

In the remaining chapters of Part One an attempt will be made to survey three avenues upon which men sought to obtain knowledge, especially a knowledge of God.

Chapter Three

KNOWLEDGE BY INTELLECT

It had been noted earlier that a new type of civilization emerged in Greece, particularly at Athens, in the fifth century. Of course, various factors were at work, paving way for what is known as the Classical Period of Greece. That which characterizes this period above everything else is the use of man's mind, rational investigations, diligent efforts to learn, a desire to expand one's knowledge.

In the fifth century B.C. Greece was a veritable beehive of intellectual activities. What a passion they had for mental pursuits. This is seen in the Greek term from which comes the English word "school," namely "σκολή" (skolay), which basically means "leisure." For many of the fifth century Athenians leisure time would be used for thinking and learning new things.[50] What a contrast with the American concept of leisure, not as a time for mental activities, but rather a time to avoid them!

The Tangible and the Temporal

The ancient Greeks had no problem accepting this present material world. Even if visible objects are seen to be imperfect copies of the unseen principles, there is no attempt to deny the existence of the object or to say they are only illusions.

In *The Republic* Plato said the Egyptians and the Phoenicians had a special love for money, but the Greeks were known for their "love of knowledge."[51] Several centuries later the Apostle Paul found the Greeks still possessing the same kind of love when he visited Athens. At the Areopagus the philosophers asked him this question: "May we know what this new teaching is that you are presenting?" (Acts 17:19, NIV) Luke then adds: "All the Athenians and the foreigners who lived there spend their time doing nothing but talking about and listening to the latest ideas" (Acts 17:21, NIV).

According to Bowra the new interest in rational inquiry among the Greeks took three forms, that of mathematics, philosophy, and natural science, appearing in this order of time.[52]

Mathematics. This subject might be treated under another heading as Plato probably would do, but for this discussion it is convenient to place it here. Babylonia and Egypt had been using mathematics earlier than Greece and it is most likely that Thales introduced it into Greece from Egypt. Plato paid a compliment to the Egyptians in regard to their mathematical skills: "Compared with the Egyptians we are childish mathematicians."[53] Hamilton concludes that the priests saw no problem with giving the Egyptians free reign in their pursuits of mathematics.[54]

It does appear that in Egypt mathematics was used more from a practical perspective, whereas in Greece it was mostly theoretical. The Greeks sought to find principles which lay behind appearances. Another important Greek mathematician was Pythagoras who believed that numbers provide the key to solving numerous problems.[55]

Although philosophy was the second important development, it will be treated later.

Natural Science. Although natural science has some overlap with both mathematics and philosophy, its methodology is different. Its emphasis is upon observation and experimentation.

The scientific method of investigation is best seen in the study of medicine which the Greeks developed in the fifth century under the direction of Hippocrates (479-399 B.C.). Detailed examination of the body involved such matters as color, temperature, appetite, taste, smell, sleep, pains, et cetera, which mark the initial work, after which the doctor could diagnose the case and prescribe a treatment.

Since the Greeks placed much emphasis upon athletic contests it was to be expected that a diligent study of the body would begin with their athletes. Aware that one's health is dependent on one's physical state of being, the Greeks were inspired to pioneer in other related fields such as anthropology, sociology, history, and geography. "They knew that human physique is relatively stable, and tried to account for rational variations by attributing them to climate or diet."[56]

One must not conclude that the new methodologies in treating physical problems were readily accepted by the populace. To the contrary, it is said that most Athenians would not submit to any other means of curing a disease than that which the temple offered.[57] In the latter part of the fifth century the sanctuaries of Asclepius were often visited by the sick.[58]

Nonetheless, the contrast struck by the Greek doctors was most obvious. In the ancient world those who were engaged in the healing of the body were often called magicians because they employed certain magical rites which were rooted in superstition. By contrast the Greeks who gave themselves to the work of healing bodies were called "physicians,"[59] because they studied nature or "φύσις" (phusis), which Glover declares was one of the greatest of the Greek words.[60] It is interesting to note that in the objective approach to medicine taken by Hippocrates he especially stressed diet and rest as remedies, for he believed nature should take its course as much as possible; thus, his adage, "Time is the great physician."[61]

The science of medicine was truly dependent upon the efforts of the philosophers to find causes behind effects. Jaeger expresses it well:

> Had it not been for the earliest Ionian natural philosophers with their quest after a "natural" explanation of all events, with their efforts to trace every effect back to its cause and to know how all the chain of causes and effects made up a necessary universal order, and with their firm belief that all the secrets of the world could be penetrated by the unprejudiced observation of things and the power of reason, medicine would never have become a science.[62]

History. Due credit should be given to the Greeks for their contributions to the field of history. These early historians embraced at least three important principles: (1) they saw that legends are not trustworthy; (2) they related a man's history to his geography; (3)

they chose prose instead of poetry as the written form of communication, which meant a clear-cut break with tradition.

It has been said that Herodotus (fifth century B.C.) carried forth the work of Hecataeus (sixth and fifth century B.C.) "on a grand scale in the true spirit of scientific investigation."[63]   When Thucydides (c. 460-400 B.C.) wrote his history of the Peloponnesian War he was careful to examine eyewitnesses and to draw conclusions only after he had thoroughly analyzed the facts.[64]

Geography. Only brief treatment is needed here. As noted earlier, geography and history have an overlap. Therefore it is easy to understand why Hecataeus became both a historian and a geographer, since personal travels were an aid to both realms. Anaximander as well as Hecataeus engaged in map drawing.

Doubtless the work of these earlier geographers was crude and lacking in many areas; nevertheless it was a pioneering effort that would ultimately stimulate further interest and advancement in an important sphere of man's life.

In assessing the innovative investigations of the ancient Greeks pertaining to this temporal, physical world one must conclude that all mankind are the recipients of multiplied blessings as a result of the direct or indirect discoveries of the Greek researchers. Edith Hamilton has summarized in a superb manner the transition of the Greek mind from the ancient to the modern world:

> To be versed in the way of nature means that a man has observed facts and reasoned about them. He has used his powers not to escape from the world but to think himself more deeply into it. To the Greeks the outside world was real and something more, it was interesting. They looked at it attentively and their minds worked upon what they saw. This is essentially the scientific method. The Greeks were the first scientists and all science goes back to them.[65]

The Invisible and the Intelligible

In this part of the chapter attention will be focused upon an area of intellectual activities that many Greeks would consider to be higher than that which pertains to the physical, material realm. Plato, in *The Republic*, identifies the two realms as (1) "the visible" and (2) "the intelligible."[66]

Philosophical knowledge. According to Bowra, philosophy followed mathematics in order of development and offered words, rather than numbers in the attempt to discover "reality behind phenomena."[67]

Jaeger identifies philosophy as "the clear perception of the permanent rules which underlie all events and changes in nature and in human life[68]" This definition reflects the importance of mental vision which Jaeger elaborates on as follows:

> The theoria of Greek philosophy was deeply and inherently connected with Greek art and Greek poetry; for it embodied not only rational thought . . . but also (as the name implies) vision, which apprehends every object as a whole, which sees the "idea" in everything—namely, the visible pattern.[69]

An important aspect of Greek thinking was to see all things in relation to the whole. The part was always seen to be relative and subordinate to the "ideal whole," whether it be in depicting art or life.[70]

The very word "philosophy" is a compound Greek term which literally means "a love of wisdom." The etymology indicates an emphasis upon the intellect. It has been said that Greek philosophy displays its strength "in its assumption that there is no problem which cannot be solved by hard and careful thought."[71]

Without question the two key men who shaped Greek philosophy were Socrates and Plato. Exactly what Socrates may have believed or taught has been the subject of debate, but M. I. Finley correctly asserts that the Socrates who really counts in shaping much of the philosophy of the West is the Socrates who appears in Plato's writings.[72] How much enlargement Plato may have given to his former teacher's presentations cannot easily be conjectured; therefore, references to one in the following discussion may well be applicable to the other.

No doubt the most important concept for both Socrates and Plato was "the Idea of Good," which is treated in detail in Plato's *Republic* 504-517.[73] In his dialogue with Glaucon, Socrates points out that there is a greater study than that of justice, bravery, sobriety, and wisdom; in fact, the greatest study of all, for Socrates, is the Idea of Good.[74]

Plato asserts that the Idea of Good is that which always does good and never does evil; it is therefore the cause of only the few things which are good.[75] In the context of this discussion Socrates is quoted as saying: "Neither, then, could God . . . since he is good, be, as the multitudes say, the cause of all things. . . ."[76]

In his discourse with Glaucon, Socrates states that in the realm of hearing there only needs to be an ear to hear and a voice to speak, without any third factor. However, in the realm of seeing it is not enough to have an eye to see and an object to be seen; there must also be a third element in order for vision to take place, namely "light." Socrates refers to the sun as heaven's deity which sends down light so that man may see visible objects in this world. Although the eye is not to be identified with the sun, Socrates does think it is "the most sunlike of all the instruments of sense."[77] Without the light of the sun one cannot see objects clearly.

An application is then made to the activities of the soul which Socrates describes in the following manner:

> When it is firmly fixed on the domain where truth and reality shine resplendent it apprehends and knows them and appears to possess reason; but when it inclines to that region which is mingled with darkness, the world of becoming and passing away, it opines only and its edge is blunted, and it shifts its opinions hither and thither, and again seems as if it lacked reason.[78]

Socrates concludes that the Idea of Good is the source or cause of both knowledge and truth; therefore it is superlative to both of them.

In the continuation of his discourse Socrates returns to his illustration of the sun and notes points of similarity and distinction in relating it to the Idea of Good. Jaeger sums up Socrates' argument in the following paraphrase:

> As the sun is the source of light, making the visible world visible, so the Idea of Good is the source of truth and meaning, and makes the thinkable world thinkable. Therefore our knowledge is not the Good, any more than our sense of sight is the sun. Yet, just as the eye is the most sunlike (helioid) of all our organs, knowledge and truth are the most goodlike (agathoid), the closest to the basic form of good.[79]

When Glaucon asked Socrates to explain himself further and to omit nothing, Socrates put forth a mathematical image to express the particular stages by which one may attain to knowledge as the highest reality. He likens progression in knowledge to a line divided into two unequal portions as follows:

Each of these sections is then divided again with the same ratio that was used in the complete line:

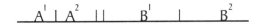

Section A represents the "visible world" while section B stands for the "intelligible world." Or, in other words, section A depicts the "world of opinion," whereas section B represents the "world of reality and knowledge." Section A^1 involves things which are only copies, such as reflections which are seen on water and shiny surfaces, or shadows cast by objects. Section A^2 covers the animal and plant kingdoms as well as all kinds of man-made objects. One can readily see that the reflections and shadows of A^1 are simply copies of the objects in A^2.

It is only in section B that one enters into a philosophical education, by moving from the area of opinion (section A) to that of truth and knowledge (section B).

Section B1 involves the specialized arts and skills such as mathematics, which comes near to the highest type of philosophical methodology used to obtain knowledge; however, mathematics cannot be in the highest area of knowledge because it is connected with the sensory realm.

Section B2 begins with hypotheses and then ascends to the "principle of the universe" or the absolute. Perhaps it would be best to have Socrates give his own comments on this section:

> Understand then . . . that by the other section of the intelligible I mean that which the reason itself lays hold of by the power of dialectics, treating its assumptions not as absolute beginnings but literally as hypotheses, underpinnings, footings, and springboards so to speak, to enable it to rise to that which requires no assumption and is the starting-point of all, and after attaining to that again taking hold of the first dependencies from it, so to proceed downward to the conclusion, making no use whatever of any object of sense but only of pure ideas moving on through ideas to ideas and ending with ideas.[80]

One can sympathize with Glaucon when he responded by saying that he understood but not fully; yet it is commendable that he grasped as much as he did, as is indicated in his own reflections which Socrates endorsed:

> I do understand that you mean to distinguish the aspect of reality and the intelligible, which is contemplated by the power of dialectic, as something truer and more exact than the object of the so-called arts and sciences whose assumptions are arbitrary starting-points. And though it is true that those who contemplate them are compelled to use their understanding and not their senses, yet because they do not go back to the beginning in the study of them but start from assumptions you do not think they possess true intelligence about them although the things themselves are intelligible when apprehended in

conjunction with a first principle. And I think you call the mental habit of geometrics and their like mind or understanding and not reason because you regard understanding as something intermediate between opinion and reason.[81]

Socrates was pleased with the presentation which he accepted as being "quite sufficient" and then he identified each of the four levels of knowledge from the highest to the lowest as follows: (1) B2 is what he calls "intellection or reason;" (2) B1 is identified as "understanding;" (3) A2 is labeled "belief;" while (4) A1 is said to be either "picturethinking or conjecture."[82]

Perhaps the clearest expression of these four stages of knowledge is given in the well-known parable of Socrates on the image of the CAVE, found in *The Republic,* 514-517. Since this mode of teaching greatly clarifies the position of Socrates, a brief survey of the parable and its application to knowledge will be presented at this point.

Socrates asked Glaucon to picture in his mind prisoners living in a kind of subterranean cave. From their childhood their legs and necks had been bound so that they could not turn their heads to ever see the direct rays of sunlight. All they could behold was the dark wall of the cave before them. Outside the cave there was light that came from a fire which burned high above and behind the prisoners. Between these captives and the fire there was a long road which had a low wall built alongside it. Men were walking upon this roadway and were transporting various kinds of tools as well as human and animal statues made from different kinds of materials. Sometimes these travelers expressed themselves verbally. By asking questions and making assertions Socrates patiently and persistently drove home his points step by step. He correctly observed that the only things the prisoners would see upon the dark café wall before them would be the images or shadows cast by light or fire upon the people and objects moving along the road. The audible sounds of the travelers would echo off the cave walls and the prisoners would doubtless think that the shadow images were in fact the speakers themselves. Consequently, Socrates concluded rightly that "in every way such prisoners would deem reality to be nothing else than the shadows of the artificial objects."[83]

Socrates then asked Glaucon to consider what would transpire if one of the prisoners were suddenly released, then required to turn about-face and start walking toward the light. The brightness of the light would bring pain to the released man who would therefore be unable to clearly discern the objects his eyes were gazing upon. If he were told that he had only seen images, reflections, and shadows on the cave wall, but now was seeing the real objects and was thus nearer to reality than before, he would probably not believe it; rather, he would doubtless hasten back into the cave to behold the reflections which he considered to be much more real to him than the blurred objects he was trying to see in the sunlit world. If, however, the man were forced out of the cave and required to climb the steep incline to the lighted world, he would need time to get his eyes adjusted and to see important relationships. It would be best for him to begin with a recognition of shadows and water reflections, after which he could then relate them to the actual objects from which the reflections came. Then he could give consideration to the appearances in heaven, first by a contemplation and observation at night, and finally, he would be able to view the sun itself in open daylight. Having reached this important summit, he would conclude that the sun is responsible for the seasons of the year and is in some way the source of visible things. If he should return to the cave, his eyes would be filled with darkness until he would not see the images and shadows clearly. If he tried to talk to the prisoners about the dullness of what he saw upon the cave wall they would declare that he had "ruined" his vision by taking a journey into the light. Moreover, if they could get released they would probably kill him.

The application is thereafter made to both the visible world and the intelligible world. Shadows, reflections, images, and appearances of tangible things fit into the world of vision, but if one would enter the intelligible world he must ascend to things higher, to the realm of contemplation. Socrates expresses this highest stage of knowledge best in his own words:

It appears to me . . . that in the region of the known the last thing to be seen and hardly seen is the idea of good, and that when seen it must needs point us to the conclusion that this is indeed the cause for all things of all that is right and beautiful, giving birth in the visible world to light, and the author of light and itself in the intelligible world being the authentic source of truth and reason, and that anyone who is to act wisely in private or public must have caught sight of this.[84]

In Book VII of his *Epistles* Plato reveals that one must work hard at the job to obtain knowledge in the highest realm.[85] Jaeger interprets Plato's discussion to mean that even the most brilliant mind cannot press its way immediately into the region of highest knowledge, but will be involved in a life-long process.[86]

Knowledge of God. William Barclay declares that in the Classical Period the Greeks were persuaded that they could obtain a knowledge of God simply by means of contemplation and intellectual processes.[87] Apparently it was assumed that there was no limit as to what the mind could grasp.

Prior to the time of Plato, Greek philosophers often identified the "highest principle in the universe," be it spiritual or material, as that which is divine or God.[88]

Jaeger notes that since the nineteenth century efforts put forth to depreciate the religious emphasis of Plato while exalting the scientific element make it impossible to understand Plato who is much more religious than those who preceded him.[89]

In the Introduction to his translation of Plato's *Republic*, Paul Shorey disassociates the Idea of Good with God: "Whatever its religious suggestions, it cannot in any metaphysical or literal sense be identified with Deity."[90] Jaeger, taking a different position, thinks that Plato does not use the name "God" for the Idea of Good, at least in part, because he could therefore differentiate between his divinity and those who made up the gods of "everyday religion."[91]

Socrates, in Book II of *The Republic*, asserts that the Good is not the cause of all things in this world because many things are evil; he then correctly adds: "Neither, then, could God . . . since he is good, be, as the multitude say, the cause of all things."[92] While Socrates does not explicitly call the Good by the name "God," it is obvious that he draws a parallel between them, which at least indicates a close relationship with one another. At any rate, it would appear that Jaeger has correctly assessed the available data when he said, "For Plato, knowledge is the guide to the realm of the divine."[93]

It is amazing that Plato reached such a high plateau of understanding relative to reality and spiritual insights without having the written Word of God. This is an excellent example of a case such as Paul relates in Romans 2:14,15 which plainly states that even if a people do not possess the written Scriptures, yet "the requirements of the law are written on their hearts" (NIV). Further revelation is found in John 1:9 where the Apostle states that Jesus is "the true light that gives light to every man" (NIV). Both of the above passages indicate a work of God wrought in behalf of all men; therefore it is an expression of divine grace. In Titus 1:11 Paul declares that "the grace of God that brings salvation has appeared to all men" (NIV).

The fact is, man is not able by his own intellect to obtain a knowledge of God in a salvation relationship. I Corinthians clearly states that "the world through wisdom did not know God" (NKJ). Paul also expressed it this way: "the natural man does not receive the things of the Spirit of God, for they are foolishness to him; nor can he *know* them, because they are spiritually discerned" (I Corinthians 1:14, NKJ).

In his discourse with Socrates Timaeus said: "Now to discover the Maker and Father of this Universe were a task indeed; and having discovered Him, to declare Him unto all men were a thing impossible."[94] It is indeed commendable that Plato gives much reference to God in the closing part of his Laws.[95] Yet, in spite of all the positive things which can be said about Plato's system, it has this obvious weakness: it is limited to only a few who can attain a philosophical education and thereby grasp the Idea of Good. The exclusiveness of such a system would of necessity leave the great mass of mankind outside the privileges of the few. It almost seems to be a predestinarian doctrine. In contrast to this position is the New Testament message that invites all men to come to Christ and know the joy of sins forgiven and a right relationship with the Creator and Redeemer.

Chapter Four

KNOWLEDGE BY EMOTIONS

A second way the pre-Christian world sought to obtain knowledge of God was by means of emotion or feeling. It has already been noted that the ancient Orient exalted the spirit of man at the expense of his mind. The world into which the New Testament came was not only affected by the intellectual breakthrough of those brilliant Greeks in the Classical Period; it was also imbued with and conditioned by the religion of the Greeks. Perhaps one should use the plural, "religions," for the Greeks were known for their sacred varieties and for the modifications and syncretisms which characterized their religious history in the millennium which preceded Christ's advent.

The Olympian Pantheon

In order to appreciate the effect of the mystery religions upon the emotions of the worshipers it is first necessary to examine briefly the popular Olympian deities.

Origin. If one would trace the development of Greek religion, he must recognize that the Greek culture is the result of the union of the Cretans to the south and the Indo-Europeans to the north, both of whom had different lifestyles.[96]

The Cretans were a peaceful, settled people who tilled the soil and harvested crops; therefore, their deities were goddesses who symbolized fertility (even as a mother gives birth to children, so Mother Earth produces crops). Throughout the Mediterranean world the fertility goddess was worshiped under various names.

The Indo-Europeans were hunters and herdsmen who lived a nomadic life. It was to be expected that they would develop deities that were masculine who displayed strength, agility, and wisdom such as were needed by the people themselves to overcome obstacles.

When these two peoples were welded into a unitary people, their religion likewise merged and produced a pantheon of both gods and goddesses. Marriage sometimes took place among the deities, such as that of Zeus and Hera.

The writings of Homer were responsible, in part at least, for the codification of the deities. Hence, Homer is sometimes called the "father of the gods." It does appear that numerous primitive deities were often united to form one Homeric god.

Characteristics. It is common knowledge that the Olympian pantheon was anthropomorphic. It is thought that the gods may have first appeared in animal form, but if so they were later transformed into a human form. According to Hamilton the Olympic Hermes was simply identified as a perfect human being, whose only mark of deity was his beauty.[97] Bowra claims that the holiness of the deities was based upon beauty and power rather than the moral quality of goodness.[98]

J. Gresham Machen observes that the Olympian deities stimulated art and literature but had no contribution to make to ethics.[99] Hamilton describes their actions as follows:

> They deceive each other; they are shifty and tricky in their dealings with mortals; they act sometimes like rebellious subjects and sometimes like naughty children and are kept in order only by Father Zeus' threat. In Homer's pages they are delightful reading, but not in the least edifying.[100]

It does seem that the gods followed their own desires without concern for good or evil, either in man or themselves.[101]

Another characteristic of Greek religion was its absence of a moral code or sacred book of authority. Consequently the door was open for much speculation. Nor did the Greeks have a great prophet. Hamilton declares that the Greek religion was not developed by prophets or priests, but by artists, poets, and philosophers.[102]

It is important that one recognize the significance of an Olympian temple; it was not a place where a congregation met to worship the deity, but rather it was essentially a dwelling place for the god or goddess. Finley comments thus:

> The rituals by which one gave thanks to the Olympic gods or pleaded with them or appeased them required no temple but an altar; and altars existed everywhere, in the homes and fields, in the places of assembly, outside the temples—everywhere, that is, but not inside a temple. One also celebrated one's gods on stated occasions by processions, games and festivals. Then the god was brought from the temple, or there might be a statue of him in the stadium or theatre; but again, nothing happened within the temple itself.[103]

Moreover, in contrast to Judaism and Christianity, there is a noticeable absence of love in the Olympian system. As a result, the gods have no problem in failing mortals during a time of crisis. For Zeus loyalty was more important than love.[104]

Specific deities. According to Arnott there are twelve deities which comprise Homer's list of gods and goddesses: (1) *Zeus,* the father and king of the gods, the lord of the sky, thunder and lightning, called by Homer the "cloud-gatherer;" (2) *Hera*, the wife of Zeus, but prior to her marriage, was known as a goddess of fertility, especially related to the city of Argos; (3) *Poiseidon*, the earth-shaker in Homer but became the sea god in the Classical Period; (4) *Hermes*, the god of the roadways, the messenger for other gods, the one who conducted the dead to the underworld; (5) *Demeter*, whose name literally means "earth-mother," was an early goddess of fertility; (6) *Artemis*, a fertility goddess, especially with the birth of both animals and humans, but later associated with wild animals; (7) *Aphrodite*, yet another goddess of fertility, who became associated with passionate sexual desire; (8) *Athena*, probably a goddess from pre-Greek times who had as one of her attributes the snake which symbolizes fertility; (9) *Hephaistus*, represented as one who was lame, may have originally been the god of volcanoes, and then at a later time became the god of those who employ fire in their labors as metal-workers and blacksmiths; (10) *Hestia*, the hearth goddess, enhancing the domestic spirit; (11) *Ares*, the war god who supposedly lived in Thrace; and (12) *Apollo*, the god of harmony, law and order as well as health.[105] The entire pantheon was accepted by the general populace, but each community had its own special patron god or goddess.[106] This deity was responsible for the security and unity of the city-state.[107] There were also divinities who were beneath the Olympians in importance and honor. Their significance lay in their relationships to local cults. Such gods as Dinonysus and Pan fit into this category.[108]

Voices of Protest

With the emergence of special interest in the intellectual realm in the sixth century it was to be expected that criticisms would be leveled against the Olympian gods and goddesses. Especially would this be true when men began to search for moral standards to mark distinctions between right and wrong.

Xenophanes of Colophon, in the sixth century B.C., wrote a stinging rebuke:

> We men have made our gods in our own image.
> I think that horses, lions, oxen too,
> Had they but hands would make their gods like them,
> Horse-gods for horses, oxen-gods for oxen.[109]

Xenophanes had a better concept of God to offer: "One God there is, greatest of gods and mortals, not like to men in body or in mind. All of him sees and hears and thinks."[110] It is indeed remarkable that Xenophanes reached such a conclusion simply by rational thought processes, apart from the written Scriptures. It would not be correct, however, to assert that it was intellectual activities alone that led him to the above position. Certainly God had written an inner law upon his heart according to Romans 2:14,15.

In the fifth and fourth centuries B.C. Socrates raised his voice against the teaching of Homer or any poet who claimed that the gods dispensed both good and evil upon mortal men.[111]

The criticism of the philosophers was partly precipitated by their efforts to explain the cause of all phenomena by just one source, which tended to stimulate an interest in monotheism or at least a "materialistic monism."[112] Angus calls the Greeks "the first higher critics" and claims that they were able to comprehend the "unity of the Deity."[113] Angus expresses the progression in this way:

> Guided by this intuition that the Divine is one, the Greek mind pursued its way through henotheism and abstract monotheism toward a truer personal monotheism which it never quite attained. Both pillars of the temple of old Hellenic religion—polytheism and anthropomorphism—fell before the assault of criticism.[114]

Perhaps Bowra was right when he suggested that the Greeks had need of the gods in order to explain what was otherwise without explanation.[115] Nevertheless, intellectual honesty went a long way in breaking down a religious system that did not and could not meet man's deepest needs.

Reference should also be made to Euripides who, in the fifth century B.C., had this to say about the activities of the gods:

> This is how we are told the gods behaved. If human beings behaved in such a way, and showed such a consistent record of deceit, cruelty and immorality, should we not reject them out of hand? Then how can we worship as superior beings gods who behave in the same way?[116]

Certainly Euripides' questions demand an honest answer.

Although the voices of protest had been raised without reprisal, by the end of the fifth century there was a strong reaction of the populace against the criticism of the intellectuals which culminated in the death of Socrates. Finley recounts the events in a vivid fashion:

> When Socrates stood trial in 399, the clerk of the court began the proceedings by reading out the indictment: "This affidavit is sworn to by Miletus . . . against Socrates. . . . Socrates is guilty of not believing in the gods in which the polis believes

and of introducing other, new divinities. He is also guilty of corrupting the young. The penalty proposed is death." The trial was completed in a single day before a jury of 501 men—all in accord with normal procedures—and he was convicted by a vote of 281 to 220.[117]

The execution of Socrates could not destroy advances made in the intellectual realm. In a general sense, then, one may say that a positive atmosphere had been created by the criticism and comments of the intellectuals. Nonetheless, one must agree with Glover's conclusion that the Greek mind was productive in most areas of pursuit, but it utterly failed in the realm of religion.[118] Is not this an excellent illustration of I Corinthians 1:21?

The Mystery Religions

One would not expect the Olympian pantheon to satisfy the deepest needs of man, especially in light of the attitudes and activities of the deities. Only time along with certain forces would continue to gnaw away at the vital core of the old religion. There were at least three elements which tended to have a destructive effect upon the polytheistic religion of Greece: (1) philosophy, (2) the destruction of the city-states, and (3) the inroads made by the Oriental religions.[119]

Arnott sums up the basic failure of the Olympians and then points forward to the need for a more satisfying kind of religion:

> The Olympian religion failed because it did not equate worship with moral responsibility. Under the Homeric scheme the believer had no stimulus to behave well, nor was there much hope of recompense in the afterlife for the virtuous man who had suffered on earth. . . .
> Thus any ritual that offered the faintest hope of such reward was assiduously cultivated, and a number of mystery cults, promising various blessings to the true believer, grew up within the context of the Olympian religion. By their nature they were destined for longer survival than the Olympian gods themselves and indeed in some ways acted as precursors of Christianity.[120]

As noted earlier, the emphasis in the Olympian system was upon loyalty, not love. Hamilton correctly asserted that Greece needed a heart religion but could not find it in Homer's pantheon.[121]

At least as early as the fourth century B.C., and perhaps much earlier, the mystical cults of the Orient gained entrance into Greece. It is quite erroneous to imagine that the Olympian pantheon was in existence for a certain period of time, then was suddenly destroyed and succeeded by the mystical, mystery religions. To the contrary, both of these types of religion existed side by side throughout a long era of time in the centuries prior to the Advent of Christ. According to Angus the "scientific and the mystical, the Olympian and the Dionysian, the philosophical and the intuitional" were contemporary with each other for a whole millennium before Christ.[122] It may be that Arnott is giving too broad an expanse of time for the mystery cults; nevertheless, it does appear that their history predates the coming of Christ by several centuries.

Dionysus. One of the earliest of the mystic cults was that of Dionysus, which apparently originated in either Phrygia or Thrace. It seems that Dionysus had originally been a fertility god represented by a bull, but later came to be known as the "god of wine."[123] Arnott describes the kind of worship as follows:

> The songs and dances in which Dionysus was worshipped became the origins of drama, and Dionysus, as well as being God of Wine, came to be heralded as God of Tragedy. . . . He is the personification of the irrational, the occasional reckless fury disregarding all reason and restraint that every man has known at some time in his life.[124]

The worship of Dionysus had some characteristics which were not found in the Olympic worship. Machen cites three, namely: (1) an immediate "contact with the god;" (2) a belief in life after death; and (3) special emphasis upon the individual.[125] With particular stress upon an intimate relationship with a god as well as a future life, one can see how many would be attracted to this kind of religion.

The overemphasis upon the emotion is seen to have played a central part in the activities of worship:

> The worshipers of Dionysus sought to attain contact with the god partly by a divine frenzy, which was induced by wild music and dancing, and partly by the crass method of eating the raw flesh of the sacred animal, the bull.[126]

When wrought up in a "state of frenzy" the worshiper of Dionysus could supposedly perform deeds beyond the power of the human.[127] Man is an emotional being and should therefore engage in religious worship which touches his emotions. But there is always a danger of developing an unhealthy situation when an undue stress is placed on any one aspect to the neglect of other equally important ones.

Characteristics. A heavy veil has remained upon the mystical cults which are known as the Mystery Religions. There is, in fact, a mystery concerning the development of these cults, which apparently began as fertility or vegetation systems.[128] Of course, there were some things, apart from the inner secret rites, that could be discussed; otherwise, there would have been little hope of attracting prospective members. The weight of evidence is such that it appears that the worshipers of the Mysteries maintained their vows to keep the inner rites a complete secret to outsiders. Consequently, it is a difficult, if not impossible, task to reconstruct the Mystery Religions in a satisfactory manner because of the limited number of extant literary sources available; added to this is the fact that these sources are necessarily limited in materials presented because of secret rituals. It is also difficult to establish an accurate chronological sequence relative to the particular changes and syncretisms which took place between the sixth century B.C. and the fifth century A.D.

According to Angus the Mystery Religions originated as a result of an awareness of the continual cycle of death and resurrection in the realm of nature.[129] It is commonly held that Attis, Adonis, and Osiris are gods of vegetation; thus their death and subsequent resurrection symbolize the yearly decay and renewal of vegetation.[130]

It does seem that the Mystery Religions used sacred drama, perhaps in the form of passion plays. No doubt William Barclay is correct when he claims that the underlying purpose of them was to lead the worshipers "to find God in emotional experience."[131] However, Barclay may be overstating the case when he adds: "They were all in the form of passion plays."[132] Machen thinks that the Eleusinian Mysteries probably had some type of religious drama.[133] Joscelyn Godwin points to a possible problem concerning such a drama at Eleusis since the renowned Telestrion room was occupied with pillars.[134] Although the question cannot be settled beyond the shadow of a doubt, it is possible that sacred dramas could have been held in some other secluded spot at Eleusis. For example, excavations at Eleusis reveal a large courtyard with "tiers of seats."[135] Perhaps passion plays were enacted in the courtyard since sufficient seating would have been available for the worshipers.

In discussing the passion plays Barclay describes what apparently took place in many of these sacred dramas just prior to the coming of Christ:

> They were all founded on the story of some god who lived, and suffered terribly, and died a cruel death, and rose again. The initiate was given a long course of instruction; he was made to practice fasting and ascetic discipline. He was worked up to an intense pitch of expectation and emotional sensitivity. He was then allowed to come to a passion play in which the story of the suffering, dying, and rising god was played out, and the worshiper identified himself with the experiences of the god . . . until he shared the god's suffering and also shared his victory and immortality.[136]

When the Greek religion of the Olympian pantheon failed to satisfy the deep inner longings of man, the Mystery Religions provided a more meaningful worship. In the Classical Period the main goal of the Greek was to live a full and joyful life, one which sought to examine all things. But that golden age was short-lived. The destruction of the city-states spelled failure for the political realm.[137] Man soon came to see that he was not sufficient to meet life's greatest problems in his own strength, nor could he simply think his way through to a proper understanding of himself, his world, and his creator. With a world crumbling at its intellectual and moral foundations the Hellenistic era from the third century B.C. onward has been aptly termed by Gilbert Murray a "failure of nerve."[138] Finding no lasting satisfaction in the things of this world, there arose a conscious need for redemption, for help from a better world.

From the third century onward the Mystery Religions claimed to be able to satisfy man's thirst for a knowledge of God.[139] A remarkable transition had taken place since the Classical Period. A gradual change in thinking resulted in the conclusion that "the γνῶσις θεοῦ [gnosis theou, knowledge of God]cannot be an acquisition of the intellect, but rather a gift of God's grace to a soul conscious of its sinfulness, and therefore, receptive of divine grace."[140]

Another important aspect of the Mystery Religions pertains to eschatology. Life and death are key matters. There is hope beyond the grave. The Greek religion had related well to the happy life, but failed to provide a message of hope and comfort for the suffering and the dying. Here is where the Mystery Religions bridged the gap and answered a felt need.[141]

According to Godwin one of the goals of the Mystery Religions was to bestow a "foreknowledge" concerning the state after death so that one would not have difficulty in entering the spirit world.[142] At any rate, one who participated in the mysteries was supposed to attain "the certitude of eternal salvation."[143]

The Eleusinian Mysteries. Before concluding this part of the chapter some references should be made to what was possibly the most famous of all the Mystery Religions, namely the Eleusinian Mysteries. This cult was founded upon the worship of Demeter, the Homeric earth mother and the corn goddess, as well as her daughter Persephone.

The interesting story of Demeter and Persephone and the founding of the temple at Eleusis is told in *The Homeric Hymns* "To Demeter." One day while Persephone and some of her friends were outdoors gathering flowers, they strayed away from the presence of Demeter.

Suddenly the earth opened and the god of the underworld, Hades, emerged with his golden chariot and immortal horses. He snatched away Persephone against her will and took her back to the underworld amidst her cries and shrieks. None of the deities heard her cries except Hecate and Helios as well as Demeter. As rapidly as an eagle Demeter moved over land and sea, searching for her beloved daughter for nine days without success. On the tenth day Hecate came to Demeter and told her that she had heard Persephone's cries but did not see who had kidnapped her. Thereafter the two goddesses hastened to Helios, who told them that Zeus had given Persephone to his brother Hades.

With bitter anguish in her heart Demeter forsook the Olympian deities and posed as an elderly lady. Making her way to Eleusis near Athens, she sat beside the city well where she met the daughters of King Celeos. They told their mother about the elderly woman they had met.

The Queen then hired her to be a nurse for her young son. Demeter took excellent care of the child and at night placed him in the fire in order to burn up his mortality and make him immortal. One night, however, the Queen saw her son placed in the fire and cried out in horror. It was then necessary for Demeter to reveal her true identity. She then urged them to build a temple for her along with an altar, and she promised to teach them her rites so that they might propitiate her.

In response to her request, the temple was built and Demeter dwelt there alone, still grieving over her lost daughter. In the meantime there were no crops growing upon earth, for famine had set in.

Out of much concern Zeus finally sent deity after deity to Eleusis to convince Demeter to return to Olympia, but she refused. Demeter declared that she would never return nor would she send fruit upon the earth until she saw her daughter.

When Zeus heard about Demeter's demands, he dispatched Hermes to the underworld to lead Persephone back into the light to be with her mother. Hades was willing to let her go at the request of Zeus, but first gave her some red pomegranate seed to eat.

Driven by the fast-moving immortal steeds, the golden chariot was soon at the beautiful temple at Eleusis. Demeter hastened to greet and embrace her beloved daughter but, suddenly gripped with suspicion, asked Persephone if she had eaten anything in the underworld and also how she had been ensnared. Persephone then recounted all that had transpired. Then Zeus sent forth Rhea to bid Demeter and Persephone to go to Olympia among the deities and also to sent forth fruit upon the earth. It was also stated that Persephone must spend one third of the year in the underworld and then the remaining two thirds with her mother. Demeter obeyed the request of Zeus and soon the earth was blooming. In the closing part of the Hymn are found these words:

> —Demeter made known
> Her holy order of service, teaching to all her most secret
> rites—
> To Triptolemos and to Polyxenos, Diocles also—
> Sacred matters to be in no way transgressed, inquired into,
> Or spoken about, for great awe of the gods makes mute the
> voice,
> Happy is he of men upon earth who has seen these wonders,
> But those uninitiated, having no part in the mysteries,
> Never share the same fate, but perish down in the
> shadows.[144]

Edith Hamilton states the worship of Dionysus underwent a modification at some point and was later introduced into the Eleusinian Mysteries:

> It was natural to associate the two—the goddess of the corn and the god of the vine, both deities of earth, the benefactors of mankind from whom came the bread and the wine that sustain life. Their mysteries, the Eleusinian, always chiefly Demeter's, and the Orphic, centering in Dionysus, were an enormously important force for religion throughout the Greek and Roman world.[145]

There were two themes, namely fertility and resurrection, which were united to bring forth the conviction that if one were initiated into the Eleusinian Mysteries he would become immortal.[146]

In the first century B.C. Cicero pays the highest compliments to the Greeks for their contribution to the Mystery Religions:

> For among the many excellent and indeed divine institutions which your Athens has brought forth and contributed to human life, none in my opinion, is better than those mysteries. For by their means we have been brought out of our barbarous and savage mode of life and educated and refined to a state of civilization; and as the rites are called "initiations," so in very truth we have learned from them the beginnings of life, and have gained the power not only to live happily, but also to die with a better hope.[147]

Perhaps the most significant contribution of the Mystery Religions pertained to the teaching of life beyond this world. Along with the emphasis upon an immediate relationship with the deity it was certain to have an effect upon the worshiper's emotions. One would expect such an experience to generally lift the spirit of the participant. It would appear that Aristophanes was thinking about this aspect of the Mystery Religions when, in his work entitled *The Frogs*, he refers to "the happy mystic bands" which is rendered "the Initiated" in another translation.[148]

Is it asking too much for all worshipers to have a mystical experience? Barclay thinks so, and claims that it is the exception and not the rule; he further asserts that only a small number are privileged to have such experiences.[149] This, of course, is a debatable point. Since the Creator made man with an emotional capacity, it is to be expected that one who is in right relationship with the Creator would have emotional experiences of some kind. At least one may more easily believe that all men might obtain mystical experiences than to believe all could reach a philosophical education.

Chapter Five

KNOWLEDGE BY VOLITION

This title needs some explanation. Perhaps it would be better to describe it as "Knowledge by Revelation," but in order to follow the headings in previous chapters the emphasis will be continued upon man's part in obtaining a knowledge of God. Revelation of God to man is indispensable if man is to come to know God; yet, in the finality of God's plan of salvation, man must activate his will in obedience to God's directions.

The last, and in many respects, the most important part of this discussion of knowledge in the pre-Christian world relates to the Jewish people. Unlike the Greeks, the Jews possessed a written propositional revelation of God in the form of what is now called the Old Testament Scripture. The Hebrews did not share the strong urge of the philosophical Greeks to examine all things in life in order to make life worth living. The Greeks of the Classical Period believed that at least some men could grasp by means of rational processes ultimate truth, being, and reality. This is not the teaching of Jewish Scripture. Nor did the Hebrews believe that man could obtain the highest kind of knowledge, that of God, simply by ecstatic emotional experiences as did the worshipers in the Mystery Religions. Judaism did not depreciate the proper exercise of man's rational powers nor the needful expression of his emotions, but it recognized the utter insufficiency of either or both of these to bring man to a genuine knowledge of God. Only by Divine revelation could God be known; if such revelation is made known it is because God has chosen to make it manifest. The thirty-nine books of the Old Testament witness to the fact of Divine disclosure to the children of Israel, and through them to other peoples.

Jehovah made it abundantly clear that He wants to be known and that He wants man to know Him. Again and again He manifested Himself in a theophany, a miraculous disclosure. Jeremiah 9:23, 24 states the most important goal possible to mortal men:

Thus saith the Lord, Let not the wise man glory in his wisdom, neither let the mighty man glory in his might, let not the rich man glory in his riches.
But let him that glorieth glory in this, that he *understandeth* and *knoweth* Me (emphasis is mine).

In the prophecy of Ezekiel is found an oft-used expression, namely, "They [or *ye*] shall know that I am God." This kind of statement appears more than sixty times. Surely this indicates that Babylonian Captivity was not only intended to break Judah away from idol gods, but to also lead them to a genuine knowledge of Jehovah.

Rational processes, physical sensations, and emotional experiences are extremely important factors in man's pursuit of knowledge pertaining to things earthly. However, when it comes to things heavenly these elements cannot span the mighty gulf between God, who is holy, and man, who is sinful. Divine revelation pointed to the way whereby man could attain a right relationship with and a true, personal knowledge of God. This way is simply by faith in and obedience toward God. The former is dependent upon the latter. Obedience makes the exercise of trust possible. Throughout the Old Testament these elements are repeatedly emphasized. Perhaps this fact is best expressed in the words of Jeremiah to the son of Josiah:

Did not thy father eat and drink, and do judgment and justice, and then it was well with him?
He judged the cause of the poor and needy; then it was well with him; was not this to know Me? saith the Lord (Jeremiah 22:15,16, KJV).

On the other hand, Old Testament Scripture declares that disobedience is the root cause of a lack of knowledge concerning God. Such disclosure of truth presupposes that there is a difference between mentally knowing about God and personally knowing Him as Sovereign Lord of one's life. Isaiah prefaced his lengthy discourse on the sinful condition of Israel with these words: "The ox knoweth his owner and the ass his master's crib: but Israel doth not know, My people doth not consider" (Isaiah 1:3). Hosea states that God had a controversy with His people "because there is no truth, nor mercy, nor knowledge of God in the land" (Hosea 4:1). In the next verse he points to their sins of swearing, lying, killing, stealing, and adultery. In verse six God said, "My people are destroyed for lack of knowledge." This destruction, however, relates to Israel's response to God's revelation: "Because thou hast rejected knowledge, I will also reject thee" (v. 6b).

In the Mosaic economy the offering of sacrificial animals was part of God's requirement for Israel, but it was not intended to be separated from an obedient heart, "For I desired mercy, and not sacrifice; and the knowledge of God more than burnt-offerings" (Hosea 6:6). Obedience is always better than sacrifice. Apart from Divine revelation and an obedient response to it, man's humanistic efforts will inevitably lead to a "failure of nerve" among any people.

Alan Richardson has summed up the Old Testament concept of knowledge in its practical setting:

> In the OT "knowledge of God" is virtually a synonym of obedience to God's will (e.g., Hosea 6:6) and to know God means to exercise lovingkindness, judgment and righteousness, as Yahweh himself does (Jeremiah 9:24). The knowledge of God's will, worship of his name, social righteousness and national prosperity; ignorance of God per contra spells disobedience, idolatry, social injustice and national disaster.[150]

The brilliant philosophers taught that man can know himself by his own intellectual strivings, but this does not square with God's Word. Jeremiah 17:9 asserts that "the heart of man is deceitful above all things, and desperately wicked" and then asks, "Who can know it?" The inference is that man does not picture himself in this manner but tends to think of himself more highly than he ought. Only God can reveal the exceeding sinfulness of sin to man's consciousness. The Psalmist was keenly aware that God knew all about him; He knew his thoughts "afar off" (139:2). He also said, "There is not a word in my tongue, but lo, O Lord, thou knowest it altogether" (139:4). In light of these facts one can well appreciate the prayer of the Psalmist in verses 23 and 24: "Search me, O God, and know my heart: try me, and know my thoughts. And see if there be any wicked way in me, and lead me in the way everlasting."

In the Hebrew text the word "yada" is by far the most oft-used term meaning "to know." This word is said to have a great variety of senses in which it is used. Nevertheless, according to W. T. Purkiser, "yada" never means to know by means of intellectual activity, but rather by means of an immediate experience.[151] "Yada" is used to describe the most intimate of all earthly relationships—that of husband and wife. "Yada signifies the knowledge of relationships between persons rather than the knowledge of logical analysis or reasoning."[152]

Perhaps one cannot stress too strongly the contribution of Judaism to the world into which the New Testament came, in terms of a right personal relationship with God as an evidence of knowing Him. Purkiser borrowed the following well-known quotation of William Temple:

> Every revelation of God is a demand, and the way to knowledge of God is by obedience. It is impossible to have knowledge of God as we have knowledge of things, because God is not a thing. We can only know a person by the direct communion of sympathetic intercourse; and God is personal. But besides this he is Creator, so that the communion of man with God is communion of creature with Creator: it is worship and obedience, or else it does not exist.[153]

Something should be stated about the intertestamental period. It appears that the rabbis were so occupied with efforts to know the Law that they failed to give proper attention to the matter of a personal relationship with God.[154] It is not strange, therefore, that at least two of the Jewish sects were legalistic.

As one surveys the pre-Christian world, he sees a flurry of intellectual activity that fails to ultimately solve his greatest problems; he also sees a frenzy in ecstatic emotional experiences whereby a worshiper of a Mystery-Religion tries to know God by imagination and feeling; but far more importantly, he sees the glorious light of Divine revelation in Judaism which pointed to a coming Redeemer, Whom to know is eternal life. When all else failed, God sent forth His Son in the fullness of time.

PART II

EXAMINATION OF SIGNIFICANT TERMS

Words are marvelous vehicles by which man is enabled to convey his thoughts. In both oral and written form, words have always played a vital part in the lives of mankind. Indeed, one would be greatly impoverished if he could neither speak, read, nor write. The purpose of this chapter is to explore various Greek words which relate to the subject of "knowledge." Special attention will be given to various verbs which mean "to know," with particular emphasis upon γινώσκω (ginosko) ἐπιγινώσκω (epiginosko), and οἶδα (oida). Discussion will also be focused upon two nouns, namely γνῶσις (gnosis) and ἐπίγνωσις (epignosis).

In surveying the early primary sources it is of interest to observe the variety of meanings employed by Homer in both *The Iliad* and *The Odyssey*. The writings of Aristophanes, Herodotus, Plato, and Xenophon are likewise informative. Of particular benefit for references to "knowledge" from the Intertestamental Period are the Dead Sea Scrolls. The *Select Papyri*, Volume I, translated by A. S. Hunt and C. C. Edgar treat such personal matters as letters, contracts, wills, receipts, invitations, etc., and date from about the fourth century B.C. to the seventh century A.D.

Although not so directly helpful in this study, the little volume *The Writers of the New Testament* by William H. Simon made at least an indirect contribution by providing many facts relative to the style, structure, and vocabulary of the New Testament writers.

E. D. Schmitz presents a helpful discussion on the development of γινώσκω and its cognates in *The New International Dictionary of New Testament Theology*, Volume II, pages 392-406. However, the most detailed work on the γινώσκω word-group is that of R. Bultmann in *Theological Dictionary of the New Testament*, pages 689-719.

Among word study sources a small volume by Donald Nash entitled *New Testament Word Studies* is instructive for ἐπίσταμαι (epistamai) and συνίημι (suniemi). *Christian Words* by Nigel Turner treats γνῶσις in a clear, albeit concise, manner. In his *Grammatical Insights into the New Testament* he discusses Christian knowledge as it relates to the Johannine literature.

It is regrettable that William Barclay in his *New Testament Words* has omitted every term for "knowledge." Likewise did R. C. Trench pass over each of the verbs meaning "to know," giving only scant treatment to γνῶσις and ἐπίγνωσις in *Synonyms of the New Testament.* Among the commentators special recognition should be given to J. B. Lightfoot, B. F. Westcott, Alfred Plummer, C. K. Barrett, and Leon Morris. Westcott gives some valuable comments on γινώσκω, οἶδα and ἐπίσταμαι in *Some Lessons of the Revised Version of the New Testament.* Perhaps the most useful commentary in the treatment of ἐπίγνωσις is *St. Paul's Epistle to the Ephesians* by J. Armitage Robinson. A very scholarly work on "Knowledge of God" appears in *The Interpretation of the Fourth Gospel* by C. H. Dodd.

In the past few years several significant essays and articles have appeared which have greatly enriched the storehouse of knowledge concerning the important word-groups for "knowledge." Donald W. Burdick has written a meaningful chapter on "Οἶδα and Γινώσκω in the Pauline Epistles" which is found in *New Dimensions in New Testament Study.* Among the numerous essays presented to F. F. Bruce on the occasion of his seventieth birthday is a stimulating article entitled "The Pauline Style as Lexical Choice: Γινώσκειν and Related Verbs" by Moises Silva in *Pauline Studies.* Equally scholarly and challenging is an article by Richard J. Erickson on "Oida and Ginosko and Verbal Aspect in Pauline Usage." This 1982 essay suggests the need to investigate some neglected areas in linguistic studies. In yet another essay Robert E. Picirelli surveys the positions which have been taken on ἐπίγνωσις, points out the strengths and weaknesses, and then adds some pertinent comments of his own that shed new light on this important Biblical term.

Meanings and Developments

In order to appreciate the various nuances of a New Testament word one must trace the history of that word in order to see how it was used in earliest records, and then note what additions and changes took place in the process of time. Not everyone agrees about the importance of tracing the historical development of a word in order to determine its New Testament meaning. For example, Richard J. Erickson suggests that the New Testament meanings of οἶδα and γινώσκω can be "reasonably established without reference to some classical norm."[1] It is difficult to understand Erickson's point since he does not elaborate on the matter, nor does he prove his point in any conclusive way. Suffice it to say that this thesis is based upon the assumption that New Testament words can best be understood in light of their historical development.

In the following chapters a historical survey of several Greek words will be sketched.

Chapter One

MEANINGS AND DEVELOPMENTS

Γινώσκω (Ginosko)

This term has generally received more attention than any of the others that bear the meaning of "know." It has been a popular word throughout its long history.

Classical usage. The long form, γιγνώσκω (gignosko), had been used from the time of Homer. The short form, γινώσκω (ginosko) appeared in the Ionic and Aeolic families, but was commonly used in literature from the time of Aristotle (384-322 B.C.) on.[2]

Liddell and Scott point out that γιγνώσκω (gignosko) was used in a variety of ways in the Classical Period, such as: (1) "come to know, perceive, . . . know by observation;" (2) "discern, distinguish, recognize;" (3) "judge, determine, decree that;" (4) "know carnally."[3]

It will help to impress upon the mind these early usages by noting quotations from primary sources. In the first instance where the verb means "perceive" or "come to know" Homer gives an example in *The Iliad*: "Now is there a work for all, and this . . . ye *know* even of yourselves."[4] (Emphasis is mine in this passage as well as in the following quotations.)

In the second group of meanings Homer also offers a clear sentence which denotes the concept "discern": "And the mist moreover have I taken from thine eyes that afore was upon them, to the end that thou mayest well *discern* both god and man."[5] In yet another translation this sentence is rendered thus: "I've cleared away the mist that blurred your eyes a moment ago, so you may see before you clearly, and *distinguish* god from man."[6] The end results are essentially the same, since in order for one to be able to clearly *discern* two beings he must be able to note the *distinctions* between them.

Herodotus affords a good example of γιγνώσκω (gignosko) when it means "judge" or "distinguish" as is seen in the following statement: "Nay, if the Spartans have now so *judged* in their anger, look to it lest at a later day, . . . they bring utter destruction upon your country."[7] Bultmann observes that γνῶσις (gnosis) is obtained in all of man's active pursuits to know, whether it be through the senses of sight or sound, or by the mental processes of examination and reflection.[8] Especially was there a close relationship between seeing and knowing as is seen in *The Odyssey*: "I *knew* it when I saw the hawk fly over us."[9]

Subsequently the mind begins to arrange the data that has been perceived by sense perceptions so that the one who has been involved in a particular experience becomes cognizant of what he has just experienced; thus γιγνώσκω (gignosko) means "experience, learn, get to know."[10] An example of this meaning is found in *The Odyssey*:

> Ah, stranger, I would that this word of thine might be fulfilled. Then shouldest thou straightway *know* of kindness and many a gift from me, so that one that met thee would call thee blessed.[11]

To this connotation in classic usage Thayer agrees. In carefully chosen language he asserts that γιγνώσκω (gignosko) "denotes a discriminating apprehension of external impressions, a knowledge grounded in personal experience."[12]

It is obvious that the Greeks considered knowledge to have a close relationship to sight.[13] One can readily see the immediate connection, for many things in daily life are known by means of sight. One knows it is a beautiful day because he *sees* the sun shining. Other senses enter the area of knowledge as well. One may also know it is a beautiful day because he *heard* his father remark that it was. Furthermore, one may know that it is a beautiful day by personally engaging in a walk outdoors and thereby *feeling* the warmth of the sun.

The term γιγνώσκω (gignosko) signifies the knowledge of what actually exists, but it also came to have the meaning of "verify."[14] The Greeks considered the eye to be a more trustworthy witness than the ear—thus verification was mainly to be accomplished by observation.[15]

Schmitz declares that γιγνώσκω (gignosko) also carries the idea of a "personal acquaintance" which results from familiar associations; the various shades of meaning are these: (1) "to know in a personal way;" (2) "to understand;" (3) "to know;" (4) "to be acquainted with, to be expert;" and (5) "to judge."[16]

Even when knowledge is obtained by consideration and reflection of facts and circumstances the element of observation is still present, as seen in the words of Thucydides: "The Epidamnians, *recognizing* that no aid was to be had from Corcyra, were at a loss how to settle their present difficulty."[17]

Noting that the object of γιγνώσκω (gignosko) may be any object of consideration, and that it can mean "to decide," "to resolve," or "to give legal recognition," Bultmann fittingly concludes that there is always to be found the element of "visual and objective verification," regardless of the shades of meaning.[18]

One further area deserves some discussion before leaving the subject of knowledge in the Classical Period. This pertains to the relationship of knowledge to truth, ἀλήθεια (alaytheia). The Greeks saw "true reality" as lying back of all earthly phenomena. While such phenomena are temporal and subject to change, the "truly real" is not bound by time but is eternal and therefore seen by ὄμμα ψυχZς (omma psuchace).[19]

For Plato all material phenomena are but the imperfect reflections of the immaterial patterns and thoughts (the ideas) by which the Creator formed the present world. Sometimes he called the ideas gods. Foremost was the idea of the Good. For Plato the highest good was to be like God.[20]

Hellenistic usage. As might be expected, the Classical usages of γινώσκω (gignosko) and its cognates carried over into the Hellenistic Period as is attested by the papyri.[21] Beyond those, however, were some new concepts in various forms of syncretistic developments that produced religious thought-systems that have been called Gnosticism.[22]

The matter of pre-Christian Gnosticism is a debatable issue. Since a subsequent chapter of this study will center on Gnosticism, further discussion will be suspended until then.

The Hellenistic Period was an important era of both transition and preparation. Especially significant was the translation of the Hebrew Scriptures into the Greek Septuagint.

Septuagint (the Old Testament translated into Greek, hereafter identified as the LXX) **usage**. According to Hatch and Redpath the term γινώσκω (ginosko) and its relatives appear about 610 times in the Septuagint with the following approximate distribution: Genesis, 37 times; Exodus, 19; Leviticus, 6; Numbers, 12; Deuteronomy, 12; Joshua, 7; Judges, 25; Ruth, 3; I Kings, 36; II Kings, 17; III Kings, 24; IV Kings, 14; I Chronicles, 6; II Chronicles, 10; Nehemiah, 7; Esther, 3; Job, 27; Psalms, 72; Proverbs, 41; Ecclesiastes, 27; Hosea, 11; Amos, 3; Micah, 4; Joel, 1; Jonah, 4; Nahum, 2; Habakkuk, 2; Zephaniah, 1; Zechariah, 6; Malachi, 1; Isaiah, 59; Jeremiah, 45; Ezekiel, 60; and Daniel, 9.[23]

A cursory observation of the above distribution reveals that the single largest unit of the Old Testament using γινώσκω (ginosko) is that of the Prophetical Books. Is not this a significant issue in light of the fact that the prophets wrote and ministered in the closing four centuries of Old Testament history? As time rushed on toward the inauguration of the New Covenant, more and more is said about knowledge, especially a knowledge of God. The second largest block of Scriptures using γινώσκω (ginosko) is the Poetical Books, while the third is the Historical Books, and finally the Pentateuch.

It is of interest to observe, as has already been noted, that in the Old Testament knowledge is often obtained by means of the senses. Verbs which mean "to hear" and "to see" are in close relationship to verbs which mean "to know."[24] In Exodus 16:6 ff. Yahweh said, "In the evening you will know that it was the Lord who brought you out of Egypt, and in the morning you will see the glory of the Lord, because He has heard your grumbling against Him" (NIV). Israel "knew" and "saw" the workings of Yahweh, and one gets the idea that He knew their state of affairs, at least from this anthropomorphic setting, because He "heard" their murmurings (see verse 12 also). Consequently, one can understand why the LXX has rendered the Hebrew verbs ra ah and hazah, which mean "see" and sama, which means "hear" by the one Greek term, γινώσκω (ginosko)[25] In I Samuel 14:38 the order is "know and see;" in Isaiah 41:20 it is "see and know."

A rapid scan of a concordance reveals that yada is by far the most oft-used verb in the Old Testament for "know," while da ath is the most-used noun for "knowledge."[26] Bultmann observes that when the Hebrew yada is translated into Greek, the terms which are most used are γινώσκω (ginosko) and οἶδα (oida), but then notes an important distinction: "Old Testament usage is much broader than the Greek, and the element of objective verification is less prominent than that of detecting or feeling or learning by experience."[27]

The Hebrew yada sometimes places an emphasis upon experience and is sometimes used in rather unique ways, such as: to know the loss of children, in Isaiah 47:8; to know grief, in Isaiah 53:3; and to know God's wrath, in Ezekiel 25:14.[28]

As already intimated, the Hebrew terms formed on the root yada have a range of meaning which denote various nuances, as in the following meanings: (1) "to notice, experience, observe," as seen in Genesis 3:7, Judges 16:20, Ecclesiastes 8:5, and Hosea 5:3; (2) "to distinguish between," as in Jonah 4:11; (3) "to know by learning," yet another possibility as revealed in Proverbs 30:3; (4) "to know how to do something" which leads to "technical ability," as seen in I Kings 7:14 and I Samuel 16:16,18; (5) "to have sexual relations with," Genesis 4:1, 19:8; (6) "to have a personal and confidential relationship with another person" (not a sexual relationship, however), Deuteronomy 34:10; and (7) in referring to man's knowledge about God, meaning his "grateful and obedient recognition, as seen in Exodus 29:45,46.[29]

Knowing God is connected with obedience to His commands. Therefore, indictment of Yahweh upon His chosen people indicates that they have deliberately chosen not to know Him by failing to acknowledge his sovereignty and right to reign over them. In their sinful living they do not know, they are ignorant of God. In Isaiah 1:3, Jeremiah 9:6, and Hosea 4:1,6 the ignorance or lack of knowledge of God is depicted. Just a casual reading of the context of each of these passages points out the corrupt condition of Israel which was the result of their own choosing. Hosea 6:1 gives an invitation to return to the Lord; verse 3 gives this admonition: "Let us acknowledge the Lord; let us press on to acknowledge Him" (NIV).

God's knowledge of man is complete and perfect. He knows man's thoughts from afar, Psalm 139:2ff. He knew Jeremiah before his body was formed in his mother's womb, Jeremiah 1:5.

C. H. Dodd asserts that God's knowledge of man has a dominant place in the Old Testament, but he has difficulty in finding man's knowledge of God.[30] Dodd further observes that the LXX has one of two ways to express man's knowledge of God: either (1) the term "God" standing as the direct object of the verb, or (2) by use of a ὅτι- (hoti) clause, as in γνῶναι ὅτι ἐγὼ κύριος (gnonai hoti ego kurios).[31]

It is also interesting to note that most of the Old Testament verses that refer to man's knowledge of God use the future tense. In commenting upon this fact Dodd writes: "Doubtless the prophets (whom God 'knew') were held to know God. . . . Yet I cannot discover a place where a prophet expressly says he knows the Lord."[32] Nor could I find a testimony to that effect. What a glorious transition as one passes to the New Testament!

In summing up the basic underlying meaning of knowledge in the Old Testament Schmitz quotes from W. A. Wolff in "Erkenntnis Gottes im Alten Testament," Ev Th 15, 1955, 426f.

> If one asks . . . for the central concept which makes comprehensible the varied uses of the one root, it is to be found in the concept of cognition. All the activities listed are merely variations on this.[33]

New Testament usage. Moulton and Geden list about 220 occurrences of γινώσκω (ginosko) in the New Testament, which have approximately the following distribution: Matthew, 20; Mark, 13; Luke, 28; Gospel of John, 55; Acts, 16; Romans, 9; I Corinthians, 14; II

Corinthians, 7; Galatians, 4; Ephesians, 3; Philippians, 5; Colossians, 1; I Thessalonians, 1; II Timothy, 3; Hebrews, 4; James, 3; II Peter, 2; I John, 25; II John, 1; Revelation, 4.[34]

Out of the 220 appearances John uses γινώσκω (ginosko) more than 80 times, which is nearly 40% of the total occurrences. Paul uses the term nearly 50 times, or about 23% of the total usages. Luke employs γινώσκω (ginosko) 44 times, or about 20% of the total number. Therefore, approximately 80% of the total occurrences of γινώσκω (ginosko) have been used by only three of the New Testament writers. In the Gospels Luke uses the term almost as much as Matthew and Mark together, while John's Gospel has nearly as many usages as the other three Gospels combined. Furthermore, in all the Johannine literature there appears nearly as many occurrences of γινώσκω (ginosko) as the Pauline Epistles and writings of Luke combined. While some may discount any particular benefit from simply counting the number of usages per writer per se, there is obviously a purpose and, therefore, some significance in the frequency with which a word is used. Certainly style, contents, and vocabulary are important factors in each New Testament book; attention will be given to these linguistic elements later on.

By far the most helpful New Testament Greek-English lexicon is that by Arndt and Gingrich which not only gives the most detailed list of meanings for γινώσκω (ginosko), but also the most detailed classification of meanings along with a well organized layout based upon grammatical structure.[35] Moises Silva commends this work for its attention to syntax and other grammatical data, but he complains that "the material is both very selective and inconsistently presented."[36] While this may be the case, it would appear that the material would have to be "selective" in order to fit into a workable volume. Unfortunately, Silva does not give an example of these supposed weaknesses.

The following discussion on shades of meaning and grammatical relations is largely drawn and adapted from Arndt and Gingrich:

1. "<u>know, come to know</u>"—(a) it is often used with the accusative case to denote something which is known, such as: the will of one's

master, Luke 12:45; truth, John 8:32; sin, Romans 7:7; love, II Corinthians 2:4; sometimes it is used to describe something which is known by something else, as in Matthew 12:33, "a tree is recognized by its fruit" (NIV). (b) The accusative case is also used to denote a personal object, such as: God, John 14:7; 17:3,25; Romans 1:21; Galatians 4:9; I John 2:3,13; 3:1,6; Christ, John 14:7; 17:3; II Corinthians 5:16; I John 2:3f. It is clear that John especially employed this latter format. (c) Often γινώσκω (ginosko)is followed by ὅτι (hoti) as in Matthew 25:24; John 6:69; 7:26; 8:52; 14:20; I John 2:3,5; 4:13; 5:2. Once again it is obvious that John is fond of this type of pattern. He often makes an assertion in this structure that marks a relationship to God. In fact he likes to speak of certitude with this pattern, "ἐν τούτῳ γινώσκομεν ὅτι" (lit., "by this we know that," I John 2:3,5; 3:24; 4:13; 5:2.)[37]

2. "Learn (of), ascertain, find out"—(a) sometimes followed with accusative case to denote the object of learning, etc., for such things as: one's circumstances, Colossians 4:8, one's faith, I Thessalonians 3:5; also used in the passive to depict that which becomes known to another, as in hidden matters, Matthew 10:26; or concerning plottings, Acts 9:24. (b) The verb is also followed by ὅτι (hoti) in John 4:1; 5:6; 12:9; Acts 24:11. Since John uses γινώσκω (ginosko) more than any other New Testament writer one would expect it to often appear in various formats, yet this particular structure seems to be a favorite of John. (c) γινώσκω (ginosko)is used in an absolute sense in Matthew 9:30 and Mark 9:30.

3. "understand, comprehend"—(a) the accusative case sometimes follows the verb to indicate the object and involves such things as: that which had been said, Luke 18:34; God's nature, I Corinthians 2:11; and the ways of God, Hebrews 3:10. (b) The verb is sometimes followed by a ὅτι (hoti) clause, as in Matthew 21:45; 24:32; Mark 12:12; 13:28f; Luke 21:30f; John 4:53; 8:27f; II Corinthians 13:6; James 2:20. It is interesting to note that this structure used in the sense of "understand" or "comprehend" is not used often by John.

(d) The verb is sometimes followed by an indirect question, and here John is the writer who uses it, as is seen in John 10:6; 13:12,28.

4. "perceive, notice, realize"—(a) Again the accusative case follows the verb to the object of perception, such as: man's wickedness, Matthew 22:18; power going out from Christ, Luke 8:46. (b) It is used in an absolute sense in Matthew 16:8; 26:10; Mark 7:24; and 8:17. (c) As usual, the verb is sometimes followed by ὅτι (hoti) as in Mark 5:29; 15:10; John 6:15; 16:19; and Acts 23:6. In the Mark chapter 5 passage is the account of the healing of the woman who had had a problem of bleeding for twelve years. As soon as she touched Jesus' clothing, her bleeding ceased and she "ἔγνω τῷ σώματι ὅτι ἴαται ἀπὸ τΖς μάστιγος" (she knew in the [her] body that she [is] was cured from the plague). Since she knew that she was healed because she no longer felt the bleeding and the pain, several versions have chosen to translate "ἔγνω" (egno) with the word "felt," namely the King James Version, Today's English Version, New International Version, Revised Standard Version, and the Jerusalem Bible.[38] The New American Standard Bible[39] and the New King James Version[40] have likewise followed the same pattern.

5. "euphem. of sex relations"—this is seen as it pertains to Joseph in Matthew 1:25 and also as it relates to Mary in Luke 1:34.

6. "have come to know, know"—(a) When the accusative case follows the verb the object may be either (1) an impersonal thing, as: truth, II John 1; sin, II Corinthians 5:21; grace, II Corinthians 8:9; all things, I John 3:20; or it may refer to (2) a person as in John 1:48; 2:25; 10:14f,27; Acts 19:15; and II Timothy 2:19. (b) The verb is followed by the ὅτι (hoti) clause in John 21:17; Acts 20:34; Philippians 1:12; James 1:3; II Peter 1:20; 3:3. (d) The verb is used with an indirect question in Luke 7:39; 10:22; John 2:25; and 11:57. (e) It is used with an adverbial modifier in Acts 21:37. (f) Finally, the verb in this classification is used in the absolute sense in Luke 2:43.

7. "acknowledge, recognize, as seen in Matthew 7:23; John 1:10; I Corinthians 8:3; Galatians 4:9.[41]

In assessing the above treatment of γινώσκω (ginosko) one may conclude that it does provide valuable insight to one's understanding of this term in the New Testament. On the negative side, however, one may justly raise a question about the significance of section 6. In analyzing various passages it is difficult to see why it could not have been treated together with section 1. Perhaps Richard J. Erickson had this in mind when he penned these thought-provoking words:

> The numerous variant glosses given in a lexicon for a word like "ginoskein"—no doubt correctly—could be organized much more effectively; and in grammars, intricate schemes of various kinds of aorist tenses—ingressive, effective, and so on—could presumably be greatly *streamlined.* (Emphasis is mine.)[42]

Other important facts concerning γινώσκω (ginosko) demand consideration but will not be discussed until later. At this time attention will be given to another important verb.

Οἶδα (Oida)

Along with γινώσκω (ginosko) this term makes up the two most important verbs for "know" in the New Testament. Οἶδα (oida) is actually a second perfect[43] of the stem "εἰδ" (eid), but it is used as a present tense.[44] Since there was no present active form εἴδω (eido), the term ὁράω (horao) was used.[45]

Classical usage. The classical writers used οἶδα (oida) in at least three different senses: (1) to see with the eye of the mind, hence, to know; (2) to know how to do something; and (3) to know that something is a fact.[46]

Homer uses οἶδα (oida) in *The Odyssey* as follows: "Phemius, many other things thou knowest to charm mortals, deeds of men and gods which minstrels make famous."[47]

The use of the second meaning is seen in the poetic lines of Aristophanes:

We will quickly make him learn
Nevermore again to spurn
Th' holy statutes of the Twain.[48]

Herodotus uses οἶδα (oida) in the sense of "knowing a fact," as seen in the following statement: "Then I would have him *know* that he was slain by his own brother."[49]

From the time of Homer ὁράω (horao), in an absolute sense, meant "to see" and "to look," but soon came to denote a spiritual seeing, in the sense of "to consider" and "to perceive;" but ὁράω (horao) was also used to denote other sense perceptions, including that of hearing (ἀκούω, akouo).[50] An active involvement in life is closely related "to seeing;" thus the connotation of experience.[51] This seems to be the meaning given by Homer in *The Odyssey*: "So he spoke, and my spirit was broken within me and I wept, as I sat on the sands, nor had my heart any longer desire to live and to behold the light of the sun."[52]

The term ἰδεῖν (idein) essentially covers the same territory as ὁράω (horao). From the time of Homer ἰδεῖν (idein) was used to express the following meanings: "to perceive," "to note," "to grasp," and also "to consider."[53]

Scholars have generally held that in the Classical Period οἶδα (oida) was used to signify knowledge which the mind grasped in a direct or intuitive manner, in distinction to γινώσκω (ginosko) which was supposedly used when knowledge was obtained by some "intermediate means" such as observation, instruction, or experience.[54] However, not all scholars are convinced that such clear distinctions held even in the Classical Period.[55]

It is reasonable to assume that in its early usage οἶδα (oida) would have borne a peculiar meaning distinct from γινώσκω (ginosko); otherwise there would be no useful purpose served in the development of new vocabulary. It is also easy to understand how a word which means "see" with one's physical eyes would be expanded into a broader context until it would thus mean "to see with the eyes of one's mind." Certainly one can relate this kind of "seeing" to an intuitive or direct knowledge.

It is important that one grasp the significance of "seeing" in its varied meanings to the Greeks and especially its religious overtones. Michaelis has expressed it well:

> The fact that there are so many verbs of seeing, and that they cover such a wide and varied range of meaning, is an indication of the high estimation of seeing (→ 316), and corresponds to its indisputable importance for man. In a very special way the Greeks were "a people of the eye." Hence it is no surprise that seeing should have taken on a very strong religious significance in the Greek world, or conversely that Greek religion may be regarded as a religion of vision.[56]

Hellenistic usage. As with γινώσκω (ginosko) one would expect classical usages of οἶδα (oida) to carry over into the Hellenistic Period, and this is true to some extent. For example, papyri dating from the third century B.C. on do reflect οἶδα (oida) as denoting knowledge in a full and absolute manner, as is seen in the following quotation given by Moulton and Milligan: "I ask you therefore not to do otherwise; but I *know* that you will do everything well."[57]

It is also to be noted that οἶδα (oida) is sometimes used in the papyri to mean "respect" or "appreciate," just as Paul uses it in I Thessalonians 5:12.[58] However, Moulton and Milligan warn that "the distinction between οἶδα (oida), 'know' absolutely, and γινώσκω (ginosko), 'come to know' . . . , cannot be pressed in Hellenistic Greek."[59]

Septuagint usage. It is interesting, if not amazing, to note that οἶδα (oida) occurs only about 240 times in the Septuagint,[60] which is considerably less than that of the total appearances of γινώσκω (ginosko), which numbered 610.[61] As will be seen later, the New Testament employs οἶδα (oida) more than γινώσκω (ginosko).

The approximate distribution is as follows: Genesis, 15 times; Exodus, 18; Leviticus, 1; Numbers, 6; Deuteronomy, 22; Joshua, 5; Judges, 4; Ruth, 2; I Kings, 16; II Kings, 14; III Kings, 11; IV Kings, 4; I Chronicles, 1; II Chronicles, 7; Esther, 4; Job, 49; Psalms, 2;

Proverbs, 11; Ecclesiastes, 8; Amos, 1; Joel, 1; Jonah, 1; Haggai, 1; Zechariah, 1; Isaiah, 16; Jeremiah, 12; Ezekiel, 1; Daniel, 6.[62]

In the earlier part of this chapter it was noted that the largest portions of scripture for γινώσκω (ginosko), in descending order, were (1) the Prophetical Books, (2) the Poetical Books, (3) the Historical Books, and (4) the Pentateuch. However, there are twice as many occurrences of οἶδα (oida) in the Poetical Books as in the Major Prophets. In the case of γινώσκω (ginosko) most appearances are in Ezekiel;[63] for οἶδα (oida) it is in the Book of Job.[64]

A unique pattern is seen in two particular passages. In Genesis 2:9 these words are found: "τὸ ξύλον τοῦ εἰδέναι γνωστὸν καλοῦ καὶ πονηροῦ"[65] which is literally saying "the tree of knowing knowledge of good and evil." The juxtaposition of these two terms indicates, at the very least, a special emphasis upon knowledge.

In I Kings (or I Samuel) 20:3 the pattern is thus: "γινώσκων οἶδεν ὁ πατήρ σου,"[66] which literally means "your father knowing knows." Obviously the stress is qualitative; thus the New International Version renders it, "Your father knows very well."

It is rather amazing that the Prophetical Books use γινώσκω (ginosko) more than any other section of the Old Testament, and yet this same division uses οἶδα (oida) less than any other section. No doubt many of the γινώσκω (ginosko) passages reflect the inceptive element of "coming to know" as is seen in Ezekiel 6:13, "And they will know that I am the Lord, when their people lie slain among their idols around their altars, on every high hill and on all the mountaintops. . . ." (NIV). It would also appear that many of the οἶδα (oida) passages denote a full, direct, intuitive knowledge, as in Job 19:25, "I know that my Redeemer lives." However, if the classical distinctions were carried through it would seem that Isaiah 26:10, "they do not *learn* righteousness," should have used γινώσκω (ginosko). At any rate, there would appear to be some interchange of terms in the Septuagint.

New Testament usage. One would probably tend to expect more occurrences of γινώσκω (ginosko) than οἶδα (oida) in the New Testament, especially in view of the Septuagint distribution. But, the fact is, οἶδα (oida) appears more often than γινώσκω (ginosko), occurring about *320* times to about *220* times for the latter.[67]

A thorough analysis of any New Testament word must not overlook the distribution rate in each. Of further value is the examination of grammatical structures or patterns in each book along with the frequency of occurrences for each. The following list presents the approximate number of times οἶδα (oida) appears in particular books: Matthew, 25; Mark, 23; Luke, 25; John, 83; Acts, 19; Romans, 16; I Corinthians, 25; II Corinthians, 16; Galatians, 3; Ephesians, 5; Philippians, 6; Colossians, 4; I Thessalonians, 13; II Thessalonians, 3; I Timothy, 4; II Timothy, 5; Titus, 2; Philemon, 1; Hebrews, 3; James, 4; I Peter, 2; II Peter, 3; I John, 15; III John, 1; Jude, 2; and Revelation, 12.[68]

One will readily note that there is an almost equal spread in the Synoptics, which was not the case with γινώσκω (ginosko). Yet the Gospel of John has more usages of οἶδα (oida) than all the Synoptics combined. Οἶδα (oida) is followed by ὅτι (hoti) 8 times in Matthew, 3 times in Mark, and 6 times in Luke. The participial form is found 3 times in Matthew, 5 times in Mark, and 4 times in Luke. The infinitive is not employed by any of the Synoptics. The use of ἵνα (hina) with the subjunctive is found at least once in each of these first three Gospels. Out of 23 usages of οἶδα (oida) Mark precedes it with the negative term, οὐ, οὐκ (not), or οὔτε (ou, ouk, oute) at least 10 times.[69]

Out of the approximately 320 appearances of οἶδα (oida) John uses the term nearly 111 times or about 34% of the total occurrences. In his Gospel where οἶδα (oida) is used about 83 times it is followed by ὅτι (hoti) at least 16 times. But much more striking is the fact that I John uses οἶδα (oida) only 15 times, yet it is followed by ὅτι (hoti) 12 times. John makes use of the participial form only 6 times in the Gospel, once in the Revelation, but not at all in the Epistles. Five times in his Gospel οἶδα (oida) is followed by πόθεν (pothen) and the verb "to be." Not once in all the Johannine literature is the infinitive used.[70] Concerning the style of John, W. H. Simcox has observed:

No sentences are attempted but such as are short, simple, and straightforward in constr., so that the writer runs no risk of going astray in them. If he has, as he very often has, more to say on a subject than will go into one short and simple sentence, he does not amplify the sentence with subordinate clauses, but dwells on or recurs to its theme in fresh parallel sentences.[71]

The Apostle Paul uses οἶδα (oida) approximately 103 times which is about 32% of the total occurrences. In other words, about two thirds of the total New Testament appearances of οἶδα (oida) are used by two writers, namely John and Paul. Paul is very fond of using the ὅτι (hoti) clause to follow οἶδα (oida); he uses this structure more than 40 times. Paul also uses the participial form over 20 times, most of which are followed by ὅτι (hoti).Unlike John, Paul does employ the infinitive, using it about 8 times. I Corinthians is similar to the Gospel of Mark in that οἶδα (oida) is preceded by οὐκ (ouk:, not) 10 times.[72]

James uses the participial form of οἶδα (oida) in two out of four occurrences in his book. Peter uses οἶδα (oida) 5 times in his two Epistles, four of which are participles.[73]

Once again, the discussion pertaining to various angles of meaning along with grammatical structure will be largely drawn from Arndt and Gingrich:

1. "<u>know</u>"—(a) it is sometimes used with the accusative case to denote a *personal object*, thus, to know a person, or to know about him, as in Mark 1:34; John 1:26,31,33; 6:42; 7:28a; Acts 3:16; 7:18; and Hebrews 10:30. It may be from a negative standpoint as in Galatians 4:8 and I Thessalonians 4:5 where it speak about those who do not know God. (b) It is also used with the accusative to depict some *thing*, as in Matthew 25:13; Mark 10:19; Luke 18:20; Romans 7:7, and I Corinthians 13:2. (c) οἶδα (oida) is also used with the accusative of a person which is then followed by a participle, as in II Corinthians 12:2. (d) Sometimes the verb is followed by the accusative and an infinitive, as in Luke 4:41; I Peter 5:9; and I Corinthians 6:2,3. (e) οἶδα (oida) is often followed by an ὅτι (hoti) clause, as in

Matthew 22:16; Luke 20:21; John 3:2; 9:31; Romans 2:2; 3:19; II Corinthians 5:1; I Timothy 1:8; and I John 3:2. (f) Sometimes it is followed by an indirect question, as in Mark 9:6; 10:38; John 5:13; 6:6; Romans 8:27; I Thessalonians 4:2; and II Timothy 3:14. (g) Sometimes οἶδα (oida) is followed by a relative pronoun, as is seen in Matthew 6:8; Mark 5:33; and II Timothy 1:12. (h) The verb is also followed by περί τινος (peri tinos), "know about something," in Matthew 24:36 and Mark 13:32. (i) Furthermore, it is used in an absolute sense in Matthew 21:27; Mark 4:27; Luke 11:44; and John 2:9b.

2. "be (intimately) acquainted with, stand in a close relation to," as in Matthew 26:72,74; II Corinthians 5:16; II Thessalonians 1:8; and Titus 1:16—obviously this goes beyond a theoretical knowledge and involves a vital personal relationship.

3. "know or understand how, can, be able"—when it bears this meaning it is usually followed with an infinitive, as in Matthew 7:11; Luke 11:13; Philippians 4:12; I Thessalonians 4:4; and James 4:17. (b) It may also be used in an absolute sense, as is the case in Matthew 27:65.

4. "understand, recognize, come to know, experience"—(a) the accusative is used to denote the impersonal object, as in Mark 4:13 and I Corinthians 2:11. (b) It may also be followed by an indirect question, as in Ephesians 1:18.

5. "remember, respect, take an interest in someone, care for someone," as seen in I Corinthians 1:16 and I Thessalonians.

In surveying other lexicons relative to the meaning of οἶδα (oida) one area of number 4 (above) stands out as being in apparent disagreement with those sources, namely the meaning of "come to know, experience." No doubt this stems from the long-standing debate as to whether γινώσκω (ginosko) and οἶδα (oida) maintain their classical distinctives in the New Testament. Since Thayer stresses the aspect of "experience" and "coming to know" with γινώσκω (ginosko) one would not expect him to relate these meanings to οἶδα.(oida)[74] Similarities and distinctions connected with these terms will be discussed later in this chapter.

Arndt and Gingrich point out that the terminology "οἴδαμεν ὅτι" (oidamen hoti) is often used to present a fact that is commonly known and accepted.[75]

W. E. Vine claims that οἶδα (oida) refers to perception and thus means "to know, to have knowledge of," in two specific ways: (1) for God it involves absolute knowledge, as revealed in Matthew 6:8,32; John 6:6,64; 8:14; II Corinthians 11:31; II Peter 2:9; Revelation 2:2,9,13,19; and (2) for man it means "to know from observation," as seen in I Thessalonians 1:4,5; 2:1; and II Thessalonians 3:7.[76]

Probably most, if not all, will acknowledge that God's knowledge is absolute and complete, but if οἶδα (oida) alone carries the idea of full and complete knowledge, how is one to view those passages using γινώσκω (ginosko) to describe God's knowledge? This, along with similar problems, demands both exploration and explanation; but, before doing so, brief discussion needs to be given to a few other Greek terms.

Ἐπιγινώσκω (Epiginosko)

This term, a compound of γινώσκω (ginosko) but not nearly as popular, has had a long history. Special attention will be focused upon New Testament meaning; nevertheless, this term deserves to have a brief survey of its meanings and development.

Classical usage. In the Classical Period there were four basic lines of meaning with some variation in each: (1) "to look upon, witness, observe;" (2) "recognize, find out, discover, learn to know, take notice of;" (3) "come to a judgment, decide;" and (4) "recognize, acknowledge, approve."[77]

Just a few references to primary sources will suffice. In regard to the first meaning Xenophon, in *Cyropaedia*, states: "And among them you would never have *detected* anyone raising his voice in anger...."[78]

Homer uses ἐπιγινώσκω (epiginosko) to express the second shade of meaning in the following statement: "I will make trial of my father, and see whether he will *recognize* me. ...."[79]

Thucydides employs the term in the sense of "find out" or "discover" in his *History of the Peloponnesian War*: "He opened the letter and in fact *found* written therein, as he suspected."[80]

In the third division which means "come to a judgment" or "decide," another passage from Thucydides is selected to denote this: "Beware, I say, lest men repudiate an unseemly sentence *passed* upon good men. ...."[81]

It does appear that ἐπιγινώσκω (epiginosko) was only sparsely used in this period. J. Armitage Robinson declares that most of the classical writers used the term from time to time, although the noun did not come into usage until the time of Alexander the Great.[82]

Hellenistic usage. Moulton and Milligan assert that the papyri would support the conclusion reached by Robinson, namely that ἐπιγινώσκω (epiginosko) "denotes not so much fuller or more perfect knowing, as knowing arrived at by the attention being directed to (ἐπί) a particular person or object. ...."[83]

In the Hellenistic Period Polybius uses the term in the sense of "recognize," "discern," or "discover," as is revealed in his statement about history: "All this can be *recognized* and understood from a general history, but not at all from the historians of the wars themselves. ...."[84] Thus it appears that this verb simply carried on the basic meaning it bore in the Classical Period.

Septuagint usage. The term ἐπιγινώσκω (epiginosko) appears about 100 times in the approximate distribution listed: Genesis, 11; Exodus, 1; Deuteronomy, 4; Judges, 1; Ruth, 4; I Kings, 1; II Kings, 1; III Kings, 1; Nehemiah, 2; Esther, 3; Job, 8; Psalms, 3; Proverbs, 4; Ecclesiastes, 1; Hosea, 4; Joel, 2; Jonah, 1; Habakkuk, 1; Haggai, 1; Zechariah, 5; Malachi, 1; Isaiah, 2; Jeremiah, 5; Lamentations, 1; Ezekiel, 29; and Daniel, 3.[85]

In tabulating this spread the Prophetical Books employ ἐπιγινώσκω (epiginosko) 55 times, or 55% of the total occurrences. The Pentateuch and the Poetical Books each use the verb 16 times, while the Historical Books use it 13 times. A random check on passages throughout the Septuagint revealed a variety of renderings for ἐπιγινώσκω (epiginosko) such as "know," "recognize," "respect," "perceive," and "understand." These renderings indicate a continuance of the basic classical meanings. As indicated in the listing, Ezekiel uses the verb far more than any other writer. An oft-used formula in Ezekiel is "ἐπιγνώσεσθε (or ἐπιγνώσονται) διότι ἐγὼ κύριος (ye or they shall know that I am the Lord)."[86]   The identity in meaning of γινώσκω (ginosko) and ἐπιγινώσκω (epiginosko) in the LXX Ezekiel is seen in the fact that the clause "ye (they) shall know that I am the Lord" uses γνώσεσθε (γνώσονται) approximately 35 times and ἐπιγνώσεσθε (ἐπιγνώσονται) about 25 times.[87]

New Testament usage. ʼΕπιγινώσκω (epiginosko) is found 44 times in the New Testament Books with the following distribution: Matthew, 6; Mark, 4; Luke, 7; Acts, 13; Romans, 1; I Corinthians, 4; II Corinthians, 5; Colossians, 1; I Timothy, 1; and II Peter, 2.[88]   The term γινώσκω (ginosko) appears 5 times more than ἐπιγινώσκω (epiginosko) and in twice the number of books.[89]

One can observe in the above listing that the writings of Luke comprise nearly half of the sum total. This verb is only found 12 times in the Pauline Epistles. What is especially surprising is the fact that John, who used both γινώσκω (ginosko) and οἶδα (oida) more than any other writer, does not use ἐπιγινώσκω (epiginosko) one time.

Lexicographers differ in their treatment of this verb. For example, Abbott-Smith does not attach the element of intensity to any of his meanings but simply comes up with a two-fold division: (1) "to observe, perceive, discern, recognize;" (2) "to discover, ascertain, determine."[90]

On the other hand, Thayer gives intensity to his first division: (1) "to become thoroughly acquainted with, to know thoroughly; to know accurately, know well;" (2) to recognize," "to perceive," "to find out, ascertain," "to understand."[91] Vine basically follows the same position as Thayer, and states that among other things ἐπιγινώσκω (epiginosko) means "fully perceive, notice attentively."[92]

Arndt and Gingrich tend to follow the pattern of Thayer and Vine but give more attention to grammar. Once again the following discussion is drawn and adapted from Arndt and Gingrich:

1. When stress is placed upon the preposition ἐπιγινώσκω (epiginosko) may mean (a) "know exactly, completely, through and through someth.," as in Luke 1:4; Romans 1:32 and Colossians 1:6. (b) "recognize, know again," as in Luke 24:16,31; and Acts 12:14. (c) "acknowledge, give recognition," as seen in Matthew 17:12; and I Corinthians 16:18.

2. When there is no stress placed upon the preposition ἐπιγινώσκω (epiginosko) basically means the same as γινώσκω (ginosko), thus—(a) "know," as in Matthew 11:27; Mark 6:54; Acts 27:39; and I Timothy 4:3. (b) "learn, find out," as in Mark 6:33; Luke 7:37; 23:7; Acts 22:29; and 28:1. (c) "notice, perceive, learn of," as in Acts 9:30; Mark 5:30; and Luke 1:22. (d) "understand, know," as in II Corinthians 1:13f and Acts 25:10. (e) "learn to know," as seen in II Peter 2:21b.[93]

Certainly it is reasonable to assume that the preposition ἐπί (epi) must bear some force, at least, as it was originally intended and used; otherwise there would have been no reason to coin the word in the first place. Thayer claims that ἐπί (epi) denotes several things when used in composition:

> 1. continuance, rest, influence upon or over any person or thing.... 2. motion, approach, direction towards or to anything. ... 3. imposition.... 4. accumulation, increase, addition.... 5. repetition. . . . 6. up, upward. . . . 7. against. . . . 8. superintendence. . . .[94]

Unfortunately, while Thayer places various compounds into the above classifications, he completely omits ἐπιγινώσκω (epiginosko). Further comments must await later discussions on distinctions.

Brief treatment will now be given to a less important verb.

Ἐπίσταμαι (epistamai)

Since this verb is not used much in either the Septuagint or the New Testament, only brief reference will be made to it.

Classical usage. Liddell and Scott list a variety of meanings, such as (1) "know how to do, be able to do, capable of doing;" (2) "to be assured, feel sure;" (3) "understand a matter,know, be versed in or acquainted with;" (4) after the time of Homer, "know as a fact, know for certain."[95]

Herodotus uses the verb in the sense of "being assured" in the following statement: "The Persians *will know* that their king is truly a man."[96]

Homer uses the verb in the sense of the meaning in (3) above as follows: "He set in the midst a woman of manifold skill in handiwork."[97]

Hellenistic usage. The papyri confirm the fact that classical usages were carried into the Hellenistic Period. Moulton and Milligan cite P Hib I.40 (B.C. 261) which reads, "You must clearly *understand*," and also P Tebt II.408 (A.D. 3) which says, "Since you *know* how I esteem and love you."[98]

Septuagint usage. Ἐπίσταμαι (epistamai) occurs about 54 times in the Septuagint with the approximate rate of distribution which follows: Genesis, 1; Exodus, 2; Numbers, 4; Deuteronomy, 7; Joshua, 4; II Chronicles, 2; Nehemiah, 1; Job, 12; Proverbs, 5; Isaiah, 8; Jeremiah, 4; and Ezekiel, 4.[99] From this spread it will be seen that the divisions using the verb, from most to least, are: (1) the Poetical Books,17; (2) the Prophetical Books, 16; (3) the Pentateuch, 14; and the Historical Books, 7.

A random check in the varied portions of the Septuagint reveals that the verb is often translated simply "know," but may also be rendered "understand," "be aware," "be skilled."

New Testament usage. The term ἐπίσταμαι (epistamai) only appears 14 times in the New Testament with the following number of occurrences: Mark, 1; Acts, 9; I Timothy, 1; Hebrews, 1; James, 1; and Jude, 1.[100] Among the five or six writers employing this word, only Luke uses it more than once. Arndt and Gingrich simply list two areas of meaning: (1) "understand τί someth.," as in Mark 14:68 and I Timothy 6:4; (2) "know, be acquainted with," as in Acts 19:15—when followed by ὅτι (hoti) it is used in Acts 15:7, 19:25; and 22:19.[101]

Thayer states that ἐπίσταμαι (epistamai) especially denotes the knowledge one obtains by being near the object known.[102] Donald Nash observes that the term means literally "to stand upon" and therefore asserts that it is

> an understanding coming from a close proximity, a knowledge which comes through practice in contrast to that gained through the processes of learning or the uncertain knowledge of hearsay.[103]

Συνίημι (Suniemi)

This is the last verb which will be given special consideration. Like the previous verb, it is not used very often in the New Testament.

Classical usage. It is mainly the metaphorical sense that concerns this study. Liddell and Scott point out that it means: (1) "perceive, hear;" (2) "to be aware of, take notice of, observe;" and (3) "understand;" yet they state the literal meaning as "set or bring together."[104]

Homer emphasizes the aspect of hearing in regard to the first meaning: "Now as he spoke fair-haired Menelaus *heard* him. . . ."[105]

In regard to the second meaning Herodotus wrote the following words which express the idea of "being aware of": "Discovering the plot, he earnestly entreated them . . . if they would but spare his life."[106]

In *The Plutus* Aristophanes gives a good example when the term means "understand": "And can't you see the meaning of the God, you ignoramus. . .?"[107]

Conzelmann asserts that συνίημι (suniemi) signifies a perception which is mainly obtained through the ear-gate and that in a broader sense it means "to note" and "to understand."[108] However, neither the verb nor the noun became part of the philosophical vocabulary.[109]

Hellenistic usage. Moulton and Milligan declare that the metaphorical sense of "perceive" and "understand" is only found in the New Testament. However, they do say that in P Cairo Zen I.59061 συνίημι (suniemi) is substituted for ἐπίσταμαι (epistamai) in the nearly parallel 59060.[110]

Septuagint usage. In the LXX συνίημι (suniemi) is found about 108 times and has the following approximate distribution: Exodus, 2; Deuteronomy, 3; Joshua, 3; I Kings, 5; II Kings, 1; III Kings, 3; IV Kings, 1; I Chronicles, 1; II Chronicles, 4; Nehemiah, 6; Job, 7; Psalms, 27; Proverbs, 7; Hosea, 2; Amos, 1; Micah, 1; Isaiah, 8; Jeremiah, 5; and Daniel, 21.[111]

The above listing indicates that συνίημι (suniemi) is found about 41 times in the Poetical Books, approximately 38 times in the Prophetic Books, about 24 times in the Historical Books, and 5 times in the Pentateuch. The fact that Ezekiel does not use this term at all is rather striking, since he used each of the preceding terms, sometimes quite profusely.

Unlike the Greek concept, the Old Testament teaches that man does not possess insight or perception as a native faculty, but rather it is God's gift, for which man should pray.[112]

New Testament usage. As one might expect, there are not many appearances of συνίημι (suniemi) in the New Testament. Moulton and Geden show about 28 uses which are found in 8 books, as follows: Matthew, 9; Mark, 7; Luke, 4; Acts, 4; Romans, 2; II Corinthians, 1; and Ephesians, 1.[113] This is the first for Matthew and the second time for the Synoptic Gospels to dominate the field relative to total usages. It is also interesting to note that John never uses the term a single time.

Out of the 28 occurrences it appears that 7 of them are quotes from the Old Testament, 6 from Isaiah. At least 8 of the usages relate to parables. Matthew uses the term 6 times in connection with parables, nearly as many as the Old Testament quotes.

In most of the New Testament passages συνίημι (suniemi) is translated as "understand," but it is sometimes rendered "be wise," "realize," and "consider."

Thayer sees συνίημι (suniemi) as meaning "to understand" in the sense "to set or join together in the mind."[114] He explains it more in detail in his discussion of synonyms dating back to classical usages. He states that συνίημι (suniemi)

> implies native insight, the soul's capacity of itself not only to lay hold of the phenomena of the outer world through the senses, but by combination (σύν and ίέναι) to arrive at their underlying laws.[115]

It appears that Thayer is taking the literal meaning in classical usages and then making application to one's ability to form mental processes. Nash probably has Thayer's comments in mind when he states that συνίημι (suniemi) means "perceive by putting together what is taken through the senses with the thinking capacity of the brain."[116] In due fairness to Thayer it must be noted that he did soften the classical meanings somewhat in applying the terms to the New Testament. To be more precise, he stated that the classical "distinctions are somewhat less sharply marked."[117]

It is not difficult to see how the ancient Greeks would formulate sensory data into an orderly pattern in the mind in order to obtain clear perception concerning a particular phenomenon. However, an acute problem develops when one tries to apply this methodology to the New Testament passages, or at least to most of them, which use συνίημι (suniemi). In the first place, the object of one's perception or understanding in the New Testament is not earthly phenomena but rather spiritual verities. Is there not something more than intellectual processes involved in the matter of apprehending and comprehending spiritual truths? I Corinthians 1:21 plainly states that "the world through its wisdom did not know Him" (NIV). Consequently, this writer has difficulty with such expressions as "native insight," "the souls' capacity of itself," and "perceive by putting together . . . with the thinking capacity of the brain," when they are linked with the συνίημι (suniemi) passages in the New Testament. Take, for example, the passage in Mark 8:14-21 where Jesus uses συνίημι (suniemi) twice. While crossing the sea in a boat, Jesus warned His disciples to watch out for the leaven or yeast of the Pharisees. Not understanding the meaning of Jesus' statement, the disciples thought it was related to the fact that they had forgotten to take bread with them. It would appear that they were "putting together" some sort of data with their brain power, but they failed to arrive at the proper perspective, for Jesus asked, "Do you still not see or understand?" (v. 21, NIV). Obviously, if only "native insight" were needed, the disciples would not have had a problem.

One must never depreciate the importance of using the rational powers he possesses, for whatever mental facilities a man may possess, although they are often called "native," are actually a gift of God. One must, in fact, use his mind to the best of his abilities in order to glorify God. While such activity is good in itself, it is not sufficient to bring one to attain a satisfying understanding of spiritual issues.

Thayer is to be commended for observing the importance of the preposition "σύν" (soon), thus the need to bring sensory data into combination *with* one's thinking powers. This writer would like to suggest another possibility relative to the significance of σύν (soon), Liddell and Scott point out that in classical usage συνίημι (suniemi) literally means "bring or set together."[118] It was often used to depict a hostile setting where men were brought together to fight one another.[119] However, it was also used, or at least came to mean "come together, come to an agreement."[120] When συνίημι (suniemi) took on a metaphorical sense it meant "perceive" with a special emphasis upon hearing.[121] Perhaps an important interpretative key is to be found in these facts. If a man is in a state of hostility toward another, his whole frame of mind would be characterized by a negative attitude toward his enemy. One in such a condition is not disposed to listen to his supposed enemy; and if he does hear him speak, it will be with a careless ear that can easily misunderstand and misinterpret. In such a state of being one will not be able to properly perceive either the words or the deeds of the one toward whom he is hostile. But how can a true understanding be obtained? Simply by reconciliation, by "coming together" no longer in hostility, but now coming together in "agreement." In this state of being one will have an ear to hear and also a mind to perceive.

Are not these principles applicable in the matter of attaining a proper understanding of heavenly doctrines in the spiritual realm? The importance of the hearing ear and the seeing eye is seen in the Mark 8:14-21 passage, but it is necessary to observe that Jesus was referring to a deeper hearing and seeing than that which could be achieved with the physical ears and eyes.

According to John 7:17 the way to obtain a knowledge of Christ's doctrine is by submitting to the will of God; in other words, by first coming into a right relationship with Christ, one will then obtain a clear perception that His doctrine is of God.

The insufficiency of man's "native insight" is seen in Luke 24:45 where we are told that Jesus "opened their minds (νοῦν) so they could understand (συνιέναι) the Scriptures" (NIV). Without a divine touch upon their minds they would not have understood the Word.

The importance of union σύν (soon, *with*) Christ in order to be a recipient of spiritual understanding is suggested in II Timothy 2:7. It will be observed that mental activity is first mentioned: "Consider what I say; and the Lord give thee understanding (σύνεσιν) in all things" (KJV). Thus one can readily see the necessity of synthesizing these two aspects of "putting together" if one is to obtain a meaning that satisfies New Testament teaching.

In light of the above facts the following conclusions are drawn. The emphases of Thayer and Nash are not sufficient to meet the New Testament connotations. Their view is too narrow and too anthropocentric, although it is good as far as it goes. A true Biblical viewpoint must emphasize both man's part and also God's part in the obtaining of understanding. Not only must man's observations and experiences be coupled together *with* his thought processes; his total being, i.e., body, mind and spirit, must also be brought into submission to God so that he might have a right relation *with* God.

Before concluding this section on "Meanings and Development," some treatment should be given to the two important nouns, namely γνῶσις (gnosis) and ἐπίγνωσις (epignosis).

Γνῶσις (Gnosis)

This is the most frequently used term for "knowledge" in both the Septuagint and the New Testament.

Classical usage. This noun was used in numerous ways, among which are: (1) "seeking to know, inquiry, investigation"; (2) "result of investigation, decision"; (3) "knowing, knowledge"; (4) "esoteric knowledge"; (5) "acquaintance with a person"; (6) "means of knowing"; (7) "being known"; and (8) "fame, credit."[122]

Since γνῶσις (gnosis) is closely related to γινώσκω (ginosko), there is no need to quote primary sources. However, it is of interest to observe that Liddell and Scott do not cite any of Homer's writings as a source for early usage of this term, which seems to suggest that it came into use after the time of Homer.[123]

Hellenistic usage. The papyri confirm the continuance of γνῶσις (gnosis) in its most general sense.[124] Moulton and Milligan cite P Hib I.92 (B.C. 263) to show that it was still used in a judicial setting, "until the *decision* of the suit."[125]

Septuagint usage. The noun γνῶσις (gnosis) is found about 45 times in the Septuagint with this approximate spread: Joshua, 1; I Kings, 1; II Kings, 1; I Chronicles, 1; Esther, 1; Psalms, 5; Proverbs, 15; Ecclesiastes, 9; Hosea, 2; Malachi, 2; Isaiah, 1; Jeremiah, 3; and Daniel, 3.[126]

In analyzing the above distribution one is impressed with the fact that the term is never used in the Pentateuch. The Poetical Books use γνῶσις (gnosis) 29 times, which is nearly 66% of the total occurrences. Of the remaining 16 occurrences only 5 are in the Historical Books. An examination of several passages from various sections of the Septuagint reveals that γνῶσις (gnosis) is usually rendered "knowledge" but is translated "understanding" on occasion.

New Testament usage. The New Testament employs γνῶσις (gnosis) about 29 times in the following manner: Luke, 2; Romans, 3; I Corinthians, 10; II Corinthians, 6; Ephesians, 1; Philippians, 1; Colossians, 1; I Timothy, 1; I Peter, 1; and II Peter, 3.[127]

Out of the total 29 occurrences Paul uses the term 23 times or 79% of the sum total. Paul makes use of γνῶσις (gnosis) 16 times in the Corinthian Epistles; this is more than half of the total New Testament appearances. Once again the omissions are rather surprising: neither Matthew, Mark, nor John uses the term a single time.

In the New Testament γνῶσις (gnosis) is generally translated "knowledge." There are references to the "knowledge of God" in Romans 1:30 and II Corinthians 10:5; "knowledge of Christ (or our Lord)" in Philippians 3:8 and II Peter 3:18; "all knowledge" in Romans 15:14; II Corinthians 1:5; 3:2; and "falsely called knowledge" in I Timothy 6:20.

Ἐπίγνωσις (Epignosis)

Although this term is not used quite as much as the preceding one, it is nevertheless an important New Testament word.

Classical usage. Liddell and Scott list the following meanings for this noun: (1) "recognition"; (2) "knowledge"; and (3) "decision."[128]

As with γνῶσις (gnosis) there are no references to Homer's use of ἐπίγνωσις (epignosis). In fact, J. Armitage Robinson declares that it was not used until the time of Alexander the Great.[129]

Hellenistic usage. This noun is found in the papyri as noted by Moulton and Milligan. In P Tebt I.28 a passage has been translated by the editors thus: "in order to prevent the details being accurately known."[130] Moulton and Milligan are not convinced that ἐπίγνωσις (epignosis) is a stronger term than γνῶσις (gnosis); therefore they question the propriety of adding the word "accurately" in the above quote.[131]

Septuagint usage. Since this noun was late coming into use, one would not expect any extensive employment in the Septuagint. The total occurrences only number 6 and are seen in these books: III Kings, 1; Esther, 1; Proverbs, 1; and Hosea, 3.[132]

It is difficult to discern any specific meaning beyond that of "knowledge" in the passages above. In Hosea 4:6 he uses both γνῶσις (gnosis) and ἐπίγνωσις (epignosis), but apparently means the same thing in both statements.

New Testament usage. This term is found 20 times in ten New Testament books: Romans, 3; Ephesians, 2; Philippians, 1; Colossians, 4; I Timothy, 1; II Timothy, 2; Titus, 1; Philemon, 1; Hebrews, 1; and II Peter, 4.[133]

Paul uses ἐπίγνωσις (epignosis) at least 15 and perhaps 16 times, if he wrote Hebrews, of the total 20 occurrences. Not only did John choose not to use γνῶσις (gnosis),he also failed to use ἐπίγνωσις (epignosis).

Usually ἐπίγνωσις (epignosis) appears as the object of a preposition. There are references to the "knowledge of God" in Colossians 1:10 and II Peter 1:2; "knowledge of the truth" in I Timothy 2:4, II Timothy 3:7, and Hebrews 10:26; "knowledge of the Lord (or the Son of God)" in Ephesians 4:13, II Peter 1:8, 2;20; and "knowledge of sin" in Romans 3:20.

Having traced the meanings and developments of these seven Greek terms, it will now be necessary to examine relationships between them.

Chapter Two

SIMILARITIES AND DISTINCTIONS

A study of synonyms is interesting, informative, and yet it is often difficult. It is usually easy to see points of likeness between terms, but it is not so easy to note their precise distinctions. In the forthcoming discussions an effort will be made to observe the possible alternatives for various combinations of terms, and then conclusions will be drawn commensurate with the findings.

Οἶδα (Oida) and Γινώσκω (Ginosko)

This is the most important combination of terms concerning which much discussion has taken place, especially during the past century or so.

Although it is not always easy to properly categorize scholars on an issue such as this, it does seem that there are three rather clearly defined groups: (1) those who assert that classical meanings do carry over into the New Testament; (2) those who deny that classical distinctions are found in the New Testament (it should be noted that not all who are classified in either group would rigidly hold to an ironclad position which would allow for no flexibility whatever); and (3) those who take a mediate view, that see various passages as maintaining classical distinctions, and yet other passages as giving no evidence whatever of a distinction.

Before identifying these positions in some detail it will be beneficial to review and further clarify the classical meanings of both οἶδα(oida) and γινώσκω (ginosko) as they are generally understood. One of the fullest descriptions is given by Donald W. Burdick:

> Whereas οἶδα [oida] was perfective, γινώσκω [ginosko] was inchoative. Οἶδα [oida] spoke of the possession of knowledge, γινώσκω [ginosko] of the acquisition of knowledge.

Οἶδα [oida] described complete and final knowledge; γινώσκωε reflecting a former state of ignorance, described knowledge as incomplete and developing. Οἶδα [oida] expressed knowledge grasped directly or intuitively by the mind, but γινώσκω expressed knowledge gained by some intermediate means such as experience, instruction, or observation. Οἶδα[oida], then, might be translated simply "I know"; γινώσκω [ginosko], "I come to know, I learn, I ascertain."

It may further be noted of οἶδα [oida]that it was used of something that was universally known or that was known assuredly. Sometimes it was employed to express "know-how," the possession of knowledge required to accomplish a desired end.[134]

As noted earlier, Richard J. Erickson questions whether classical usage made these kinds of distinctions, at least in the Greek of Plato.[135] Nevertheless, in this study the above distinctions will be assumed to have held true in the Classical Period, since many notable scholars would tend to accept a clear line of demarcation in the classics. If there were no distinctions in the Classical Period, it is indeed strange that Thucydides used both verbs in his *History of the Peloponnesian War* in the following sentence: "But once let them learn [γινώσκω, ginosko] that you are aware [οἶδα,oida]. . ."[136]

Classical distinctions affirmed. J. B. Lightfoot, that renowned scholar of the nineteenth century, placed the weight of his great name behind this position. In commenting upon I Corinthians 2:11 which uses both Greek verbs (except in the Textus Receptus) Lightfoot states that "οἶδα (oida) 'knoweth' denotes direct knowledge, while ἔγνωκεν (egnoken) 'discerneth' involves more or less the idea of a process or attainment."[137] Lightfoot clearly asserts the maintenance of the classical meanings in I John:

> The examination of the passages, where the two words are found in the First Epistle of St. John, shows most clearly that they were employed with the same precision of meaning as in the classical age. While οἶδα [oida] is simple and absolute,

γινώσκω [ginosko] is relative, involving more or less the idea of a process of examination. Thus, while οἶδα [oida] is used of the knowledge of the facts and propositions in themselves, γινώσκω [ginosko] implies reference to something else, and gives prominence to either the acquisition of the knowledge or the knowledge of a thing in its bearings."[138]

Another reference by Lightfoot will further shed light on his understanding of these two Greek verbs. In Galatians 4:9 γινώσκω (ginosko) is used, whereas οἶδα (oida) had been used in verse 8. According to Lightfoot γινώσκω (ginosko) is preferred over οἶδα (oida)

> (1) where there is reference to some earlier state of ignorance, or to some prior facts on which the knowledge is based; (2) where the ideas of "thoroughness, familiarity," or of "approbation," are involved: these ideas arising out of the stress which γινώσκω [ginosko] lays on the process of reception.[139]

For Cremer γινώσκω (ginosko) expresses "an active relation . . . of the knower to the object of his knowledge," whereas οἶδα (oida) expresses "a relation of the object to the subject."[140]

When B.F. Westcott discusses I John 2:3, he states that when a knowledge of God is obtained by means of experience, γινώσκω (ginosko) is used; but when that knowledge is absolute and immediate, οἶδα (oida) is used.[141] In his comments on John 2:24 he declares:

> It is of great importance to distinguish in the narrative of St. John the knowledge (1) of discernment and recognition, from that (2) of intuition and conviction. The one word (γινώσκειν) implies movement, progress: the other (εἰδέναι) satisfaction, rest.[142]

One will observe that Lightfoot and Westcott particularly maintain that the classical distinctions are found in Johannine writings. A detailed study of οἶδα (oida) and γινώσκω (ginosko) in the Gospel of John (1959) by Ignace de la Potterie draws the same conclusions as did

Westcott.[143]   This essay, written in French, claims that John uses the terms in their distinctive classical usage. Erickson thinks that Potterie reached his conclusions without giving proper attention to the facts and therefore "forces some evidence, ignores other, and more than once completely begs the question at issue in order to make his point."[144]

A number of other scholars fit into this first classification, such as F. L. Godet, Alfred Plummer, Archibald Robertson, A. E. Brooke, Marvin Vincent, A. T. Robertson, William Hendriksen, R. C. H. Lenski, and John R. W. Stott.[145]

See Appendix A for a more detailed discussion by Westcott.

Classical distinctions denied. The earlier viewpoint held that classical meanings are employed in the New Testament. However, a change of opinion developed among various scholars in the twentieth century. For example, in 1928 John H. Bernard made the following statement in his commentary on the Gospel of John: "It is doubtful if the two verbs can be differentiated with any precision."[146] Moulton and Milligan insist that the distinction which Lightfoot makes between οἶδα (oida) and γινώσκω (ginosko) cannot be pressed in Hellenistic Greek."[147]

In recent years other notable scholars have embraced this position. C. H. Dodd, in his work entitled *The Interpretation of the Fourth Gospel*, says: "Whatever difference of meaning the two words may originally have shown would seem to have practically disappeared by our period."[148] Heinrich Seesemann takes virtually the same position in the TDNT when he states that "in the koine it is hard to establish any distinction of meaning."[149]

Leon Morris questions whether one can assert classical distinctions, especially in the Gospel of John.[150] He correctly observes that Bernard has presented a strong case against maintaining the classical meanings and then cites Bernard's comments on John 1:26 as follows:

> Both verbs are used of Christ's knowledge of the Father; γινώσκω [ginosko] at 10:15 and 17:25, οἶδα [oida] at 7:29 and 8:55. Both are used of the world's knowledge (or ignorance) of

God, or of that possessed by the Jews: γινώσκω [ginosko] at
1:10, 17:23,25; 8:555, 16:3, I Jn. 3:1,6; οἶδα [oida] at 7:28, 8:19,
15:21. Both are used of man's knowledge of God and Christ:
γινώσκω [ginosko] at 14:7,9; 17:3; I Jn. 2:4,13,14; 4:6,7,8; 5:20,
and οἶδα [oida] at 1:31,33; 4:22; 14:7. Both are used of Christ's
knowledge of men or ordinary facts, e.g., γινώσκω [ginosko] at
2:25; 5:6,42; 6:15; 10:14,27 and οἶδα [oida] at 6:64; 8:37; 13:3.
The word used for the Father's knowledge of the Son is γινώσκω
[ginosko] (10:15), and not οἶδα [oida] as we should have
expected. With this array of passages before us, we shall be
slow to accept conclusions which are based on any strict
distinction in usage between the two verbs.[151]

It would appear, at first sight at least, that Bernard has dealt a
devastating blow to the advocates of the first position who claim that
classical distinctions are maintained in the New Testament. Certainly
his clear presentation of several categories where both Greek terms
are used in each category furnishes a strong argument in favor of aban-
doning the position that classical meanings are still extant in the New
Testament. However, an examination of all the verses in each of the
above categories does raise some questions which demand a response.
First of all, in regard to man's knowledge of both the Father and the
Son, John 14:7 is cited as using both verbs. Actually, γινώσκω
(ginosko) is used twice, while οἶδα (oida) is used once. The verse
reads thus: "If you really knew (γινώσκω, ginosko) me, you would
know (οἶδα, oida) my Father as well. From now on, you do know
(γινώσκω, ginosko) him and have seen him" (NIV plus Greek terms).
While it is clear that John chose to use both terms, is it possible that he
did so for a purpose, rather than to simply use the words interchangeably for the sake of variety? Could it be at all possible that John was
trying to say something of this sort: "If you had really come to know
Me by personal experience, you would have immediately and directly
known my Father, but from this point on you are coming to know Him
because you are seeing Him in Me." Neither Bernard nor Morris
appears to have given any consideration to this possibility.

Concerning the passages which refer to Christ's knowledge of men
or of common facts, one may well ask whether Christ's humanity has

import here. Discussion in Mark chapter 13 centers on the return of Christ and the end of the age. Jesus said, "No one knows (οἶδα, oida) about that day or hour, not even the angels in heaven, *nor the Son,* but only the Father" (NIV with added Greek term). Does not this statement reveal the fact that Christ laid aside at least a portion of His omniscience during His earthly ministry? If so, what effect might the Incarnation have had on the use of γινώσκω (ginosko) in the New Testament? Obviously, this possible solution has also been ignored by the advocates in this second camp.

Consider, for example, John 5:42 which employs γινώσκω (ginosko). Is it possible that Jesus' knowledge about those who did not have God's love in their hearts was based, for His emphasis here at least, upon His successive observation of their evil deeds which betrayed a lack of that love? The context will support such an assumption. Westcott says that Jesus knew "by the knowledge of experience."[152]

In John 10:14 Jesus said, "I know (γινώσκω, ginosko) my sheep and my sheep know (γινώσκω, ginosko) Me" (NIV). Perhaps Jesus means that He has come to know His disciples, at least in one sense, as a shepherd comes to know his sheep, namely by observation of and experience with them. If this is the case, γινώσκω (ginosko) has been purposefully chosen.

Admittedly, John 6:15 cannot be treated so easily. It does not appear that Jesus received by intermediate means His knowledge that men were coming to force Him to become king. On the other hand, there is nothing in the context that would prohibit such means.

John uses γινώσκω (ginosko) in 10:15 to express the Father's knowledge of the Son. Bernard declares that one would have expected οἶδα (oida) to be used here. His conclusion seems to be correct until one examines the verse in its context. Verse 14 has been discussed above where Jesus said, "I know my sheep and my sheep know Me." Verse 15 states that "the Father knows (γινώσκω) Me and I know (γινώσκω) the Father. If verse 15 is taken entirely by itself, it would appear that γινώσκω, (ginosko) is completely out of place as far as classical distinctions are concerned. Of much importance in this passage is the little word καθώς (kathos, as), which connects and relates verse 15 to verse 14. If one can accept the analogy in verse 14 that Jesus knows His own followers in the same way a shepherd knows his sheep, the presence of οἶδα (oida) seems to demand that γινώσκω (ginosko) be used in both clauses in verse 15. If John were trying to emphasize the Father's knowledge of the Son in respect to progressive relationships throughout Jesus' earthly life from childhood to adulthood, would he not need to use the term γινώσκω, ginosko), if indeed there were distinctions in the Classical Period and they were carried over into the New Testament?

Although Bernard has put forth a noble argument, he has not proven conclusively that οἶδα (oida) and γινώσκω (ginosko) mean exactly the same thing, that they are used interchangeably as variants one of another.

C. K. Barrett and Nigel Turner also fit into this second classification.[153] While Turner notes some characteristics of both οἶδα (oida) and γινώσκω (ginosko), he emphatically wrote: "Classical distinctions no longer hold in the New Testament."[154]

Before leaving this section reference should be made to Matthew 7:23 and Luke 25:12. In Matthew 7:23 Jesus said, "I never knew (γινώσκω) you" (NIV). In Matthew 25:12 He said, "I don't know (οἶδα) you" (NIV). Seesemann says it is difficult to find any difference of meaning in these two verses.[155]

Nash disagrees with such a conclusion and bases his position upon a distinction between οἶδα (oida) and γινώσκω (ginosko) which we have not yet discussed. He claims that

> Ginosko implies some relationship between the knower and the object known, whereas, oida simply indicates that the person or object known has come within the knower's area of perception.[156]

He bases this statement on Thayer's comment that γινώσκω (ginosko) expresses "a discriminating apprehension of external impressions, a knowledge grounded in personal experience.[157] In applying this distinctive to the above passages Nash states that in Matthew 7:23 Jesus was only saying that "the person had never come into an approving relationship of personal intimacy," whereas Jesus' statement in Matthew 25:12 "is a sharper rebuke suggesting that the person is not even within the scope of the Lord's perception."[158] Since he does not elaborate further, it is difficult to see the force of his argument. The comment on 7:23 is understandable from the classical standpoint, but the second comment is not convincing. When Peter denied Christ in Matthew 26:72 he said, "I don't know (οἶδα (oida) the man!" (NIV). Surely Peter did not mean that he had no perception of Christ in any manner. Rather, as the context indicates, he meant that he did not have a personal, intimate relationship with him. Consequently it would seem best to consider οἶδα (oida) and γινώσκω (ginosko) interchangeable in both of these verses.

Mediate position. A third position avoids the extremes of the above two. On the one hand, this viewpoint does not deny the usage of classical meanings in the New Testament; but on the other hand, it does not affirm that all the occurrences fit into the mold of clear-cut classical distinctions.

This mediate position recognizes that there are passages which are similar if not identical in content that apparently use οἶδα (oida) and γινώσκω (ginosko) interchangeably. For example, Jesus said in Matthew 16:3, "you know (γινώσκω) how to interpret the appearance of the earth and sky" (NIV). One cannot see any basic difference in the words of Christ in Luke 12:56, "you know (οἶδα) how to interpret the appearance of the earth and the sky" (NIV).

James 1:3 reads, "you know (γινώσκω) that the testing of your faith develops perseverance: (NIV). When one compares this verse with Romans 5:3, it is difficult to see any essential difference: "we know (οἶδα) that suffering produces perseverance" (NIV).

One more example will suffice. Οἶδα (oida) and γινώσκω (ginosko) are both used in Romans 7:7, "I would not have known (γινώσκω) what sin was except through the law. For I would not have known (οἶδα) what it is to covet if the law had not said, 'Do not covet'" (NIV). This is a very clear reference made up of parallel statements that are strikingly similar, yet employing different verbs for "know." In this usage it is quite obvious that both terms mean exactly the same thing.

A contemporary scholar who fits into this third category is Donald W. Burdick, who wrote a chapter on "Οἶδα and Γινώσκω In The Pauline Epistles" for *New Dimensions in New Testament Study* (1974).[159] Burdick begins with the assumption that οἶδα (oida) and γινώσκω (ginosko) had clear-cut distinctions in the classical usage, but he does not assume that these distinctions were continued in New Testament times by the Apostle Paul; in fact, he claims that his purpose is to examine Paul's use of the two verbs in order to find out if the classical distinctions are being preserved.[160]

In his inductive study Burdick approaches οἶδα (oida) and γινώσκω (ginosko) from three different aspects: (1) he examined every one of the 153 occurrences of these verbs in the Pauline Epistles within its context with these questions in mind; "Does this passage more naturally support the classical meaning of the verb used, whether οἶδα or γινώσκω, or does it more naturally indicate that the verbs were used interchangeably?"; (2) he then examined those passages where each verb was used in "close proximity" to the other one, by asking the same kind of questions; (3) Burdick finally analyzed those passages which were "similar but separate" by asking the above questions.[161]

Richard Erickson finds fault with Burdick's methodology because it opens up too much "to the student's own intuition," and therefore may result in opposite conclusions depending upon one's interpretation.[162] Erickson does not see any significance in relating New Testament verbs to classical meanings (he has serious questions as to whether these verbs had any distinctions in classical times); rather, he suggests asking this question, "How are they related to each other in the NT?"[163]

Erickson correctly warns of the danger of intuitive and subjective elements in competent interpretation, yet he errs by lightly dismissing the relationship of New Testament words to earlier classical meanings, be they real or supposed. It is to be feared that he may be leaning too much to subjective aspects in drawing his conclusion at this point.

In all fairness to Burdick he did examine each verb; not simply in its verse, but in its context. This factor adds some objectivity to his methodology. Furthermore, Burdick observes Paul's use of ἵνα (hina) with both verbs, as well as the use of the infinitive of purpose.[164] The conclusion of the entire study is summed up by Burdick as follows:

> In summary, of the 103 occurrences of οἶδα in the Pauline Epistles, 90 were used with the classical meaning, 5 were judged to be equivocal, and 8 were used with the same meaning as the classical γινώσκω. Of the 50 occurrences of γινώσκω, 32 were used with the classical meaning, 8 were judged to be equivocal, and 10 were used with the same meaning as the classical οἶδα.[165]

From the above conclusion it will be noted that Burdick sees 18 out of 153 occurrences as denoting equivalent meanings where the verbs are used interchangeably.[166] Burdick has correctly rejected the viewpoint that the Greek verbs οἶδα (oida) and γινώσκω (ginosko) are always used with distinctive classical meaning, but he also properly rejects the opposite viewpoint that the terms are no longer employed with classical distinction.[167]

Lexical stylistics. In a 1980 publication Moises Silva presented a very interesting and informative study on "The Pauline Style as Lexical Choice" in which he discussed γινώσκω (ginosko) and other related verbs as well.[168] Silva states his purpose thus: "to propose a method for the investigation of linguistic, specifically lexical, patterns with a view to determining their relevance for exegetical decisions."[169] Convinced that style plays an important part in the matter of interpretation, Silva is particularly anxious to examine the stylistic patterns in the vocabulary of the Pauline Epistles, especially with οἶδα (oida), γινώσκω (ginosko) and other related verbs.[170]

An evaluation of style is dependent upon two vital areas of study: (1) "syntagmatic relations," by which he means syntactical collations or combinations; and (2) "paradigmatic relations," by which he means the potential vocabulary that was available to Paul for the expression of certain statements.[171] One can readily see the significance of applying these principles of general linguistics to a study of New Testament synonyms in order to determine semantic distinctions.

Unlike many prior investigations of synonyms, Silva chose a broad range of terms, including antonyms as well. In classifying the verb usages he chose the following divisions: (1) active voice where the verb rules the direct object; (2) patterns using the passive voice; (3) active voice where the verb rules a clause (not including relative clauses); and (4) cases where the verb is used in an absolute sense.[172] It will be noted that various grammatical structures are treated under some divisions.

An examination of Appendix C will reveal that in Section III, item (1), οἶδα (oida) plus ὅτι (hoti) appears far more frequently than does γινώσκω (ginosko) plus ὅτι (hoti). Silva claims that οἶδα (oida) plus ὅτι (hoti) seems to be "largely predictable" and should not, therefore, be held to bear a distinctive meaning.[173] Silva is apparently accepting Warren Weaver's assertion that information is directly related to one's freedom to choose his words when giving a message, which Silva expresses in this manner: "If there is no uncertainty whatever—if the message is totally predictable—there is no choice in the selection of the message and thus the message carries no information."[174] An example cited is the use of clichés which are usually considered "stylistically weak" simply because they are used often and, consequently, are rather predictable. By the expression "stylistically weak," Silva means "they carry less 'information' or 'mean' less."[175] Although Silva recognizes exceptions to the οἶδα + ὅτι (oida + hoti) pattern in the occurrences of γινώσκω + ὅτι (ginosko + hoti), he declares that there are only three of the passages in the latter pattern that ought to be decided on a semantic basis.[176]

In his treatment of Romans 8:28, "And we know (οἶδα) that in all things God works for the good of those who love him" (NIV), Burdick concludes that οἶδα (oida) was used because the passage bears the classical connotation of assurance.[177] In contrast to this viewpoint Silva thinks Paul chose οἶδα (oida) here as well as in verses with similar patterns because of "stylistic, rather than semantic, reasons."[178]

By way of assessment one may say that Silva is to be commended for his efforts to determine meanings of synonyms by means of stylistic patterns. While his conclusions are not given in a dogmatic fashion, they are not altogether convincing. As he himself concedes, more exploration and "refinement" are needed in order to provide a clear objective aid.[179] There are two other points on which Silva is helpful. In his so-called "proximity passages" Burdick sees no reason for the use of both οἶδα (oida) and γινώσκω (ginosko) in Romans 6:6,9: thus he concludes the two terms are used interchangeably.[180] Verse 6 reads, "Knowing (γινώσκω) this, that our old man is crucified with Him" (KJV), while verse 9 states, "Knowing (οἶδα) that Christ being raised from the dead dieth no more" (KJV). Silva wisely notes a syntactical reason for the verbal change, namely the use of τοῦτο (touto, *this*) in verse 6.[181] One other reason may be added for using γινώσκω (ginosko) in verse 6, simply that of personal experience. Burdick rejects this suggestion as given by Charles Hodge and claims that Hodge was assuming that γινώσκω (ginosko) always reveals knowledge gained by experience, instruction, or observation.[182] Burdick denies that one can experience the crucifixion of his old self and thereby reveals a theological prejudice in spite of the clear teaching of Scripture.[183]

One more "proximity passage" is worthy of notice, Galatians 4:8,9: "Formerly, when you did not know (οἶδα) God, you were slaves to those who by nature are not gods. But now that you know (γινώσκω) God—or rather are known (γινώσκω) by God" (NIV). Burdick questions the use of γινώσκω (ginosko) in the last statement since God's knowledge is always absolute and direct; but then he justifies Paul's use of γινώσκω (ginosko) by stating that the Apostle was expressing a knowledge of persons, not of facts.[184] This is hardly a convincing argument. Silva wisely notes that Paul had no choice of terms since οἶδα (oida) is never used in the passive.[185]

Another factor which must not be overlooked in the New Testament usage of οἶδα(oida) and γινώσκω (ginosko) is the matter of "semantic neutralization." Silva gives needed warning: "Semantic distinctions which are drawn on the basis of convincing examples must not be generalized, as is usually done, without paying due attention to the possibility of semantic neutralization."[186] Perhaps this would explain various passages where οἶδα (oida) and γινώσκω (ginosko) are apparently used interchangeably. Further exploration is needed in this area.

Verbal aspect. Before closing the discussion on similarities and distinctions between οἶδα (oida) and γινώσκω (ginosko) some reference should be made to a recent study on "Oida and Ginosko and Verbal Aspect in Pauline Usage" by Richard J. Erickson.[187] The following comments will involve a brief summary and evaluation of Erickson's viewpoint.

Commendation should be given to Erickson for seeking a new objective-type approach to the study of synonyms. His emphasis is placed upon the verbal perspective of "aspect" or kind of action which he places into three divisions: (1) "imperfective," which refers to progressive, repeated action; (2) "perfective," which expresses action that is completed, thus a state; and (3) "neutral," which does not specifically mark the action either way.[188] Numerous verbs reveal all three aspects, but γινώσκω (ginosko) and οἶδα (oida) only seem to display two and one respectively, as indicated in the following chart produced by Erickson:

IMPERFECTIVE ASPECT (process) present stem	AORIST ASPECT (neutral) aorist stem	PERFECTIVE ASPECT (state) perfect stem
Manthanein "to be learning"	Mathein "to learn"	Memathekenai "to have learned" (=to know)
apothneskein "to be dying"	apothanein "to die"	tethnekenai "to have died" (=to be dead)
———	gnonai "to know"	egnokenai/ginoskein "to know"
——	——	eidenai "to know" [189]

Unfortunately, Erickson does not offer a clear presentation as to how he has arrived at the above positions, nor does he give descriptive Biblical examples which use οἶδα (oida). In the examples which he discusses, Galatians 2:7-9, Colossians 4:7,8, I Thessalonians 3:5,6, and Romans 1:19-21, an aorist participle or infinitive of γινώσκω (ginosko) appears in one clause which relates to another or parallel clause which has a verb in either the indicative or participial mood. In the last three of these examples Erickson sees the verbs opposite to γινώσκω (ginosko) as having "to do with the impartation of information" while the aorist of γινώσκω (ginosko) in the other clause "has to do with the receiving (or even the active gathering) or [sic] information."[190]

Erickson claims that the aorist neutral aspect of γινώσκω (ginosko) is used for the imperfective aspect, apparently basing this conclusion on the context of Galatians 2:1-10 which deals with the investigation made of Paul by the Apostles at Jerusalem.[191] This leads to Erickson's next chart:

IMPERFECT ASPECT	AORIST ASPECT	PERFECTIVE ASPECT
gnonai "to come to know"	gnonai "to know"	egnokenai/ginoskein "to know"
——	——	eidenai "to know"
idein? "to come to see/perceive"	idein "to see"	blepein? eidenai?! "to see, to have come to see=to know?"[192]

In drawing a conclusion concerning his findings Erickson states that

for certain contexts these two verbs are indeed used synonymously. But ginoskein, with its richer aspectual possibilities, can be used in the sense of acquiring knowledge;

whereas, eidenai, restricted to the perfective aspect, cannot. This perhaps is what has given rise to the impression that the two verbs represent different kinds of knowledge. No evidence for that contention has come out of this study, however.[193]

Erickson's work is difficult to follow. In order to clarify his positions he needs to build more bridges to explain how he gets from one point to another. He should give examples using οἶδα(oida) as well as γινώσκω (ginosko). Verbal aspect may shed new light on the old problem of meanings in οἶδα (oida) and γινώσκω (ginosko), but it would appear that added research needs to be made if this perspective is to be more meaningful.

Γινώσκω and Ἐπιγινώσκω
(Ginosko and Epiginosko)
Γνῶσις and Ἐπίγνωσις
(Gnosis and Epignosis)

Since most commentators recognize ἐπιγινώσκω (epiginosko) as differing from γινώσκω (ginosko) at least in some passages, this discussion will focus upon key positions taken on ἐπιγινώσκω/ ἐπίγνωσις (epiginosko/epignosis).

Intensive knowledge. This is probably the most popular view taken by commentators. There is little doubt that J. B. Lightfoot's contributions on this word has affected many scholars in the past century. In his comments on Philippians 1:9 Lightfoot identifies ἐπίγνωσις as "advanced, perfect knowledge," and refers to ἐπί (epi) as an "intensive preposition."[194] In his discussion on Colossians 1:9 he gives a more complete explanation:

> The compound epignosis is an advance upon gnosis denoting a larger, more thorough knowledge .... Hence also epignosis is used especially of the knowledge of God and of Christ, as being the perfection of knowledge.[195]

Another advocate of this viewpoint is William Barclay who says that ἐπίγνωσις (epignosis) can mean either "increasing knowledge" or "full knowledge."[196] Noting that the preposition ἐπί (epi) means "toward, in the direction of," Barclay concludes that ἐπίγνωσις (epignosis) may therefore refer to "knowledge which is always moving further in the direction of that which it seeks to know."[197]

Directive knowledge. Among those who differ with Lightfoot is J. Armitage Robinson who has written what may be called a "classic" treatment upon another viewpoint:

> If now we inquire what is the force of the preposition, or in other words how does ἐπιγινώσκειν differ from γινώσκειν, we may note first of all that the simple verb would have given the meaning, intelligibly if less precisely, in all the cases which we have cited. There is no indication that ἐπιγινώσκειν conveys the idea of a fuller, more perfect, more advanced knowledge.
>
> We find a large number of compounds in ἐπί, in which the preposition does not in the least signify addition, but rather perhaps direction. It seems to fix the verb upon a definite object. . . . In these cases we cannot say that the compound verb is stronger than the simple verb. The preposition is not intensive, but directive (if the word may be allowed). It prepares us to expect the limitation of the verb to a particular object.
>
> Thus γινώσκειν means 'to know' in the fullest sense that can be given to the word 'knowledge': ἐπιγινώσκειν directs attention to some particular point in regard to which 'knowledge' is affirmed. So that to perceive a particular thing, or to perceive who a particular person is, may fitly be expressed by ἐπιγινώσκειν. There is no such limitation about the word γινώσκειν, though of course it may be so limited by its context.[198]

At the close of his treatment on ἐπίγνωσις (epignosis) Robinson draws these conclusions:

> So far then as we are to distinguish between γνῶσις and ἐπίγνωσις, we may say that γνῶσις is the wider word and expresses 'knowledge' in the fullest sense: ἐπίγνωσις is

knowledge directed towards a particular object, perceiving, discerning, recognizing: but it is not knowledge in the abstract: that is γνῶσις.[199]

Penetrating knowledge. H. A. W. Meyer is an exponent of this position. He claims that ἐπίγνωσις (epignosis), at least in its usage in Colossians denotes "knowledge which grasps and penetrates into the object."[200]

Ingressive, decisive knowledge. Robert E. Picirelli chooses Robinson's viewpoint as being more convincing and better supported than that of Lightfoot.[201] However, Picirelli thinks that both of these earlier scholars overlooked an important factor. Picirelli argues that since ἐπί (epi) added to γνῶσις (gnosis) gives a literal meaning of "knowledge-upon," ἐπίγνωσις (epignosis) in many of its usages has "an inceptive force, referring to the specific experience when one came to the knowledge of some person or thing."[202] He sees ἐπίγνωσις (epignosis) in this setting a "punctiliar" word which denotes a "crisis experience" whereas γνῶσις (gnosis) would often be a "linear" word which expresses a condition or state of existence.[203]

It does appear that Picirelli draws a correct conclusion when he states that, when ἐπι (epi) is added to γνῶσις (gnosis), it "makes a specific application of the word to a specific situation or circumstance."[204] It is interesting to observe that he does not entirely discount the intensive aspect given by Lightfoot.[205]

Intensive, directive knowledge. Leon Morris unites these two elements in his discussion of ἐπιγινώσκω (epiginosko) as is seen in his comments on I Corinthians 13:12:

> The use of the compound verb often signifies no more than that one's knowledge is directed towards (epi) a particular object. But it may have the thought of a full and complete knowledge and would seem to have the force of it here.[206]

B. C. Caffin takes virtually the same position but enlarges upon the directive aspect:

Ἐπίγνωσις is a stronger word than γνῶσις; it means "knowledge" directed towards an object, gradually approaching nearer and nearer to it, concentrated upon it, fixed closely upon it. So it comes to mean the knowledge, not merely of intellectual apprehension, but rather of deep contemplation; the knowledge which implies love for only love can concentrate continually the powers of the soul in close meditation upon its object.[207]

An assessment of the above viewpoints is not an easy task. In light of the various New Testament usages one may correctly assert that each of the writers has made a valid contribution to a better understanding of ἐπιγινώσκω/ἐπίγνωσις (epiginosko/epignosis). However, no single position will meet the varied contexts of the New Testament; therefore, it is suggested that a collation of each aspect is necessary to give a complete coverage.

Γινώσκω and Ἐπίσταμαι
(Ginosko and Epistamai)

In Acts 19:15 γινώσκω (ginosko) is contrasted with ἐπίσταμαι (epistamai), "Jesus I know (γινώσκω) and Paul I know (ἐπίσταμαι)." Various suggestions have been offered. R. J. Knowling thinks that γινώσκω (ginosko) may especially express knowledge which is personal, whereas ἐπίσταμαι (epistamai) seems to denote knowledge of a fact.[208] Lightfoot rendered the verse thus: "Jesus I acknowledge and Paul I know."[209] On the other hand, Nash says that the meaning may be that the evil spirit had a closer relationship with Paul than with Christ; knowing Paul by a personal acquaintance or contact but knowing Jesus only by means of His power.[210]

It is very difficult to differentiate between these verbs, at least in the above context. Perhaps it is best to judge them as equivocal.

Οἶδα and Ἐπίσταμαι
(Oida and Epistamai)

These two verbs appear together in Jude 10, "Yet these men speak abusively against whatever they do not understand (οἶδα); and what things they do understand (ἐπίσταμαι) by instinct . . . these are the very things that destroy them." Most commentators do not bother to discuss the verbs. Nash claims that οἶδα (oida) refers to "natural knowledge" while ἐπίσταμαι (epistamai) expresses "acquired knowledge"; yet he admits that this would mean changing the order in Jude.[211]

Once again it appears very difficult to make any clear-cut distinction in this setting.

Ἐπίσταμαι and Συνίημι
(Epistamai and Suniemi)

The term συνίημι (suniemi) is often translated "understand" but ἐπίσταμαι (epistamai) can also be translated by the same word. Perhaps both terms overlap to some degree with the other synonyms for "know."

Donald Nash notes this difference, however. He declares that ἐπίσταμαι (epistamai) denotes knowledge gained by way of exercise orpractice while συνίημι (suniemi) expresses knowledge that is obtained by means of hearing and learning activities.[212]

Conclusions

Throughout Part II assessments have been made concerning word meanings, grammatical constructions, and conflicting viewpoints of scholars. It is now in order to form, by way of summary, conclusions that have been derived from the perspective of the whole.

1. There is solid evidence that classical distinctions for various terms are carried over into New Testament usages in many passages. This conclusion is supported by both contextual and syntactical relations.

2. There are also clear cases where the terms do not bear a distinct meaning one from the other, but are used interchangeably, perhaps for no other purpose than to provide variety. Syntagmatic and paradigmatic relations are doubtless significant factors in this area.

3. It must also be admitted that there are usages which are difficult to determine. In some cases it would appear that more than one nuance would fit a given context. Certainly dogmatism is to be avoided in such instances.

4. The principles of general linguistics have been applied to Biblical literature with beneficial results. Only the surface has been touched thus far. Consequently there is a vast area open for investigation, both intensive and extensive in such areas as lexical stylistics, morphological gaps, syntagmatic and paradigmatic relations, and semantic neutralization processes.

PART III

KNOWLEDGE IN THE NEW TESTAMENT

As one reads the New Testament, he is impressed with repeated references to "knowledge." Both Paul and John often use various Greek verbs meaning "know." However, as noted in Part II, the Apostle John never uses the noun forms γνῶσις (gnosis) or ἐπίγνωσις (epignosis). These nouns are mainly employed by Paul.

Although the New Testament does use the verb "know" and the noun "knowledge" in a variety of ways, the particular interest of this thesis is upon man's knowledge of God. Surely the greatest knowledge obtainable by man is tersely stated by Paul in Ephesians 3:19a thus: "to know the love of Christ, which passeth knowledge."

Part III will focus attention upon five aspects of knowledge, namely (1) Gnosticism; (2) knowledge by nature; (3) knowledge by the Word of God; (4) knowledge through Christ; and (5) knowledge through the Holy Spirit.

Chapter One

GNOSTICISM

No meaningful discussion of New Testament "knowledge" can possibly bypass the unique phenomenon known as Gnosticism. In December of 1945 one of the most important archaeological finds of the twentieth century was uncovered in Egypt near the town of Nag Hammadi. The discovery was indeed accidental since the two peasants were only seeking to find fertilizer; but how providential a dig it was. In this important find were brought to light the sacred writings of various movements known as Gnosticism which apparently were founded sometime after the inception of Christianity.[1]   Prior to the 1945 discovery, except for a couple of the early Gnostic documents, scholars have had to depend upon the refutation of the Church Fathers who treated the Gnostics as heretics. Doubtless the Fathers were at times unfair in their polemical treatment; nevertheless, A. D. Nock is probably correct when he states that they have given us "the bone structure" of Gnosticism, to which the Nag Hammadi writings have placed "much more flesh."[2]

Just a little more than one year later, in early 1947, the first of the Dead Sea Scrolls were found in a cave at Qumran. This important discovery was destined to overshadow the finds at Nag Hammadi and thus dominate the attention of scholars for the next couple decades. With the translation of the Nag Hammadi writings into English in the nineteen seventies a renewed surge of interest has been stimulated in behalf of Gnostic studies.

Meaning of Terms

In a meaningful discussion of any subject it is imperative that there be an agreement on the meaning of terms; otherwise, there will always be misunderstanding, misinterpretation, and confusion. Unfortunately, New Testament scholars are not united in the precise meaning of the terms "Gnosticism" and "Gnostic." F. F. Bruce asserts that the etymology of the terms is not the deciding factor in unfolding the meanings, but it is rather the way the terms are used.[3]

Robert Grant notes that the etymology of Gnosticism indicates that the Gnostic has knowledge; however, this knowledge has not been obtained by learning processes, but by revelation which has been given to him.[4]

Jacques Lacarriere points out the diversity of meaning for "Gnostic" in the following comments:

> The term Gnostic is vague, encompassing several distinctively different meanings. But, historically speaking, it acquired a particular meaning during the early centuries of our era. On the Eastern shores of the Mediterranean, in Syria, Samaria, and Egypt, at the moment when Christianity was feeling its way, and when so many prophets and messiahs were travelling the high roads of the Orient, founding short-lived communities here and there, certain men called Gnostics, that is to say "men who know," were also setting up important communities, grouped around various masters and female initiates of a teaching that was radically different from all the others.[5]

There are essentially two camps that have emerged in the ongoing debate as to the meaning of Gnosticism: (1) those who adhere to a narrow definition which does not make room for a pre-Christian Gnosticism, and (2) those who use a broad definition that sees Gnosticism not only in the New Testament but also in other early writings as well.[6] The advocates in the first camp think Gnosticism can best be accounted for by the influence of Christianity, while those in the second camp suggest just the opposite, namely that the New Testament has resulted because of the influence of pre-Christian Gnosticism.[7]

F. F. Bruce wisely concludes; "When two such directly opposed positions can be held, we may suspect that the evidence is ambiguous, or that powerful a priori factors are at work."[8]

Generally speaking, the German scholars headed by Bultmann have embraced a broad definition; whereas British and American scholars have tended to accept a narrow meaning which usually limits Gnosticism to a Christian heresy in the second and third centuries A.D.

Origin

Not only is it difficult to define Gnosticism; it is perhaps even more difficult to pinpoint its origin. Grant notes that there are four theories that have found a rather broad acceptance, namely, from: (1) the ancient religions of the Orient, such as Indian, Mesopotamian, or Zoroastrian; (2) unorthodox Judaism; (3) unorthodox Christianity; and (4) philosophy in the late Hellenistic Period, particularly Neoplatonism.[9]

It does appear that Gnosticism as fully developed in the third and fourth centuries A.D. was indebted in some respects to contributions made by the Mystery Religions. S. Angus expresses it this way:

> The Mystery-Religions were systems of Gnosis akin, and forming a stage to, those movements to which the name of Gnosticism became attached. They professed to satisfy the desire for the knowledge of God which became pronounced from at least the second century B.C. and increased in intensity until the acme of syncretism in the third and fourth centuries of our era.[10]

Likewise Richard Reitzenstein sees Gnosticism as an outgrowth of the Mystery Religions.[11]

The military conquests of Alexander the Great effected a blending of Oriental and Occidental beliefs which resulted in a syncretism that had great influence, directly or indirectly, upon the world into which the New Testament came.

> But the fundamental passion for God and the corresponding attraction of esoteric knowledge are features which tend to recur in all Oriental faiths: and as the latter were modified by, and in turn reacted on, Hellenic culture and philosophy, the resulting syncretism or fusion of belief and practice gave birth to a rich, bewildering progeny of strange speculations,

purificatory and expiatory rites, and mysteries, in which magic and cabbalistic formulae and cryptic signs played a part.[12]

Characteristics

The fact that there were many varieties among the advocates of Gnosticism adds further difficulty in listing characteristics of these movements. A. D. Nock was keenly aware of the problems involved and therefore stated that "an adequate discussion of the general theme of Gnosticism would require more than human powers of knowledge and of sympathy."[13] R. McL. Wilson points out general characteristics in *The Gnostic Problem* as follows:

> The characteristic of Gnosticism in all its forms is syncretism, blending together elements of every sort, and finding room for every type of thought, from the highest philosophical mysticism to the lowest forms of magic. There is in consequence no one uniform set of ideas that may be singled out as Gnostic; rather is it a matter of a type of thought which manifests itself in different ways in different groups. Yet there are certain characteristic features which reappear in different forms and combinations in the different systems, ideas assimilated from various sources and not always co-ordinated into a consistent scheme.[14]

Although the Gnostics constructed their teachings from numerous sources, Lacarriere thinks it is proper to identify Gnosticism as "a profoundly original thought, a mutant thought."[15] Whatever differences may be held by scholars there are certain characteristics which reflect the basic tenets held by Gnostics in general: (1) God is transcendent; (2) a problem that needs to be solved pertains to the existence of evil in this world; (3) a suggested answer to this problem is that the world was not created by God but by a demiurge who is sometimes said to be the Jehovah of the Old Testament; (4) in some men is to be found a "spark of divinity" which enables them to make a response to God's revelation and thereby be able to someday return to the divine abode beyond this material world; (5) mankind are often arranged in a three-fold classification, namely (a) the spiritual, (b) the psychic, and (c) the material—the first two alone are said to be able to attain salvation; (6) the knowledge obtained is received, not primarily by means of rational processes, but rather by means of revelation.[16]

One can readily see that there is a great gulf between God and the material world, including man's physical body. The important part of man is the "I," the "self" or "the divine spark" within him which is alien to his material body. Werner Foerster makes reference to this dualistic aspect of man by portraying an image which he calls "gold in mud"— the gold referring to the "I" and the mud to the body from which the self longs to be freed.[17] Foerster describes the obtaining of Gnosis in the following manner:

> The central factor in Gnosis, the "call," reaches man neither in rational thought nor in an experience which eliminates thought. Man has a special manner of reception in his "I". He feels himself "addressed" and answers the call. He feels that he is encountered by something which already lies within him, although admittedly entombed. It is nothing new, but rather the old which only needs to be called to mind. It is like a note sounded at a distance, which strikes an echoing chord in his heart. Here is the reason why the basic acceptance of Gnosis can and should take place in a single act.[18]

It is not strange, therefore, that two kinds of Gnostics emerged, both holding to a position which despised matter, especially the human body. On the one hand, there were those who became rigid ascetics, having as little to do with this present world as possible. On the other hand, there were those who went to the other extreme and became antinomians, giving themselves to all kinds of licentious living on the basic assumption that only the spirit really matters.

Schmitz sums up the concepts of Gnosticism by noting that it expresses "a manner of life which sprang from a denial of the validity of human existence in history and the cosmos. It found expression for its beliefs in a syncretistic mythology, and expressed itself in the negation of ethics."[19]

Alleged Evidence for Pre-Christian Gnosticism

Advocates of a pre-Christian Gnosticism tend to base their position on the supposed support of various sources. Only a few of the more important ones can be discussed.

The Church Fathers. As noted earlier, some scholars have questioned the validity of the polemical writings of the Church Fathers. While allowances must be made for over-statements resulting from over-reactions or a lack of careful inquiry, one must remember that the Fathers were contemporary with the Gnostics. Therefore, as S. Petrement rightly concludes, they had as full a knowledge of the Gnostics as we do.[20]

It is well known that the Church Fathers applied the name "Gnostic" first of all to Simon whose teaching was called "Simonianism." From the time of Irenaeus to Eusebius the Fathers taught that Simon was the originator of all heresy.[21]

Jean Danielou thinks that the Simonian type of gnosis might properly be labeled as "pre-Christian Jewish Gnosticism."[22] Many cannot accept Simon as a full-fledged Gnostic, however. One of the objections brought forth is that the Acts of the Apostles does not designate Simon as a Gnostic, but rather as a magician.[23]

In assessing the teaching of Simon, Wilson sums it up in the following manner:

> It is clear from this brief survey that Simon's system is nothing more nor less than an assimilation of imperfectly understood Christian doctrines to a fundamentally pagan scheme. Something is due to Stoicism, something to the Orient, something to Christianity, but the Christian elements play a relatively small part. Several features of later Gnostic thought are already present (unless they have been read back into the theory), such as the conception of emanations, the idea that the world is the creation of inferior powers, and that there is in it an element of the divine imprisoned and awaiting deliverance. These views are foreshadowed in earlier thought, and it seems

that Simon is simply another charlatan after the manner of Alexander of Abonoteichus and his kind. . . . Such elements of Christianity as are present are largely superficial, and there is no sign of any true conception of the message of the Gospel. It is subordinated to flights of fancy, while the antinomian strain at once cuts Simon off from the essentially Christian line of thought as it is presented by Paul and the Church.[24]

Certainly one cannot establish positive evidence for a fully developed Gnosticism in the movement known as Simonianism.

Nor can one prove that the epistles written by Ignatius between A.D. 108-117 present a full-fledged Gnosticism. Scholars in the "History of Religions" School have often claimed that they have found Gnostic elements in and Gnostic influence upon the writings of Ignatius. Virginia Corwin takes issue with such conclusions and declares that the opponents of Ignatius reveal only an elementary form of Gnosticism at the most, for at that time "there was no clear-cut single movement that could be defined as Gnostic, certainly not of a Mandaean sort, but there were, rather, varieties of thought . . . more properly . . . called protognostic."[25]

Hermetic Literature. These writings were produced in Greek and found in Egypt upon manuscripts which date from the fourteenth century and later.[26] Although many scholars would date the Hermetica in its original composition to as early a time as the second century A.D., Dodd thinks that the first tractate known as "Poimandres" was possibly written even earlier; for he declares that "there is no evidence which would conflict with a date early in the second century or even late in the first century."[27]

Reitzenstein claimed that a sect associated with "Poimandres" was inaugurated about the time of Christ. From this tractate he constructed a "Gnostic Redeemer myth" wherein the Primal Man or the Anthropos manifests himself as a redeemer.[28] A powerful critique has been written by C. Colpe which reveals that the Anthropos does not act as a redeemer in "Poimandres."[29]

Yamauchi asserts that the three most outstanding scholars of the Hermetic literature declare that it was written between the second and fourth centuries and then he cites the comments of Munck:

> There have in fact been attempts in the past to prove the pre-Christian nature of Gnosticism by dating Gnostic writings in the period before the New Testament writings were composed. This was attempted, for instance, in the case of the Hermetic literature, which, however, was finally proved to be later.[30]

Mandaeism. The Mandaeans represent a Gnostic sect that has survived to the present time in both Iran and Iraq. It is difficult to summarize the doctrines of this movement because it lacks the uniting thread of consistency: "It is neither consistently monotheistic nor consistently dualistic. But in its main intention it is based upon a dualism not unlike that of the Manichees."[31]

Oscar Cullman thinks that the Mandaeans were a Baptismal sect from Palestine which influenced the followers of both John the Baptist and Christ.[32] Certainly this is a presumptuous conclusion to draw in light of the fact that extant literature probably cannot be dated earlier than about the eighth century. Stephen Neill correctly notes that the original writings doubtless harken back to an earlier date, but how much earlier is not known, perhaps back to the second century.[33]

C. H. Dodd rejects the suggestion that the Mandaean literature provides solid support for a pre-Christian Gnosticism; he expresses it thus: "But alleged parallels drawn from this medieval body of literature have no value for the study of the Fourth Gospel unless they can be supported by earlier evidence."[34]

Judaism. Various scholars have been impressed with clear references to the Old Testament in the Coptic texts found at Nag Hammadi, especially those that point back to the early chapters of Genesis. On this basis it is held by some that pagan Gnosticism originated "as a development of Jewish Gnostic exegesis of Genesis."[35]

The Dead Sea Scrolls have led some to believe that these writings are proof of pre-Christian Gnosticism. There are indeed numerous references to knowledge in the DSS.

W. D. Davies has placed the main passages which treat knowledge in the DSS into six classifications in which da'ath or its relatives convey the following shades of meaning: (1) a rational discrimination or perception; (2) a close affinity to the Law; (3) an esoteric or secret knowledge; (4) an eschatological meaning or an explanation of unfolding events; (5) a warm, personal type of knowledge; and (6) a transmitted knowledge.[36]

Only one passage will be cited in each of these classifications. Concerning rational discrimination one may cite DSD III:2 as an example: "and his understanding and powers and possessions shall not be brought into the Council of the Community."

A reference which has close association to the Law is seen in DSD III:1, "For his soul has loathed the teachings of knowledge, he has not established (within him) the ordinances of righteousness by conversion of his life."

An example in the third classification which relates to a secret type of knowledge is found in DSD IX:22, "He is to bear unremitting hatred towards all men of ill repute, and to be minded to keep in seclusion from them."

In regard to eschatological meaning DSD XI:3 states, "For from the fountain of His knowledge He has opened my light, and mine eye has beheld the wonders He has done and my heart is illumined with the Mystery to come."

A passage which depicts a personal type of knowledge is seen in DSD XI:6, "My eye beheld wisdom: because knowledge is hidden from men and the counsel of Providence from the sons of men."

Mediated knowledge is expressed in DSD X:23, "With thankful praises I will open my mouth; and the righteous acts of God shall my tongue relate continually."[37]

Many other passages could be cited in the DSS which reveal much emphasis upon knowledge. It is difficult, if not impossible, to prove that there was a pre-Christian Gnosticism found in the Qumran community. It may be argued that the evidence is actually to the contrary, that there may have been no direct Gnostic influence upon Judaism in Palestine prior to the Advent of Christ in light of basic differences in soteriology, anthropology, cosmology, and ethics.[38]

A strong point against accepting the assumptions of certain writers that Gnosticism was an element in the Qumran literature is the testimony of students of Bultmann who have come to different conclusions from that of their teacher. Both K. G. Kuhn and Hans Jonas have chosen to disassociate the DSS with Gnosticism.[39] M. Wilcox endeavors to treat the issue fairly:

> Was the sect at Qumran a Gnostic one? If we restrict the meaning "gnostic" to "having to do with secret knowledge of the mind and will of God," perhaps we may be led to answer yes. But if we are looking for a way of salvation expressed in terms of some kind of knowledge apart from Torah and "deeds in Toray," or for the presence and activity of a redeemer-revealer figure, historical or mythological, or indeed an emphasis on knowledge in its own right, we shall have to say no.[40]

The important factor is seen to be the way one defines "Gnosticism." It does seem best to refrain from any identification of the DSS with Gnosticism as an organized system.

According to K. Rudolph both Christianity and Gnosticism sprang forth out of "Jewish Gnosticism."[41] Danielou asserts that the original gnosis harkens back to Jewish Christian theology, from which the Gnostics borrowed ideas and then adapted them to fit their dualistic systems.[42] Furthermore Danielou concludes that "Gnosticism as a system is fundamentally foreign both to Judaism and to Christianity," but he also notes that Gnosticism developed into a "Christian heresy through the intermediate influence of heterodox Jewish groups."[43]

In the final analysis one may say that those who contend for a pre-Christian Jewish Gnosticism lack conclusive evidence for their position. Yamauchi sums up the alleged support and draws a significant conclusion:

> When we review the evidences which have been adduced to prove the existence of a truly dualistic Jewish Gnosticism, we find that the sources are either ambiguous or late, or both. For example, such early sources as the Apocrypha, Philo, the Dead Sea Scrolls, and the New Testament itself do not reveal clear-cut cases of Gnosticism. The Colossian heresy clearly

betrays Jewish elements, but it cannot be shown to be Gnostic beyond dispute. This does not, of course, deny the possibility or even the probability that such Jewish-tinged Gnosticism may have existed. What is not proven, however, is a full-fledged pre-Christian Gnosticism.[44]

Gnosticism and the New Testament

In light of the fact that some New Testament scholars have presupposed the emergence of Gnosticism prior to that of Christianity, one would expect them to interpret the New Testament against the backdrop of a Gnostic system. In such a frame the New Testament is often reviewed as being part of a two-fold development: (1) the first stage involves the earlier Books which supposedly employ Gnostic concepts, whereas (2) the second stage relates especially to the later Books which tend to protect against Gnosticism.[45]

Brief attention will be given to the various divisions of the New Testament. The viewpoint of those who hold to a pre-Christian Gnosticism will first be presented, and then a response will be given.

The Gospel of St. John. In the Introduction to R. Bultmann's commentary on the Gospel of John (English translation) W. Schmithals expresses a relationship between the Fourth Gospel and Gnosticism:

> On the one hand John manifests close contacts with the Gnostic conception of the world. The source of the discourses, which John takes over, or to which he adheres, is Gnostic in outlook. It has its closest parallels in the Mandaean writings, the oldest strata of whose traditions go back to the time of primitive Christianity and to the region of Syrian Palestine. In these Mandaean revelatory addresses are also to be found parabolic sayings that characterize the Revealer as the good Shepherd, the real Vine, etc. Moreover, the Gnostic Odes of Solomon are especially closely related to the discourses of John as are the Letters of Ignatius of Antioch, whose Christology shows itself strongly influenced by a Syrian Gnosticism. In John Jesus descends from heaven, like the Gnostic Redeemer, to bring to men the saving message, and he returns to the

Father after completing his work. In face of his word light and darkness separate themselves; before him life and death are decided. He who is of the truth hears his voice; to the blind, however, the messenger of life remains hidden.[46]

It is obvious that the contrasting elements mentioned by Schmithals are seen in a Gnostic setting. But is this the only possible interpretation? Opposites are mentioned from the earliest pages of Holy Scripture. Why should one be limited to a supposed system of pre-Christian Gnosticism as a background from which the Gospel of John was penned? For Bultmann to assert that the writer of John's Gospel had been converted from a Baptist Gnostic sect is pure conjecture.[47]

W. F. Albright takes issue with Bultmann concerning a late dating for the composition of the Johannine writings:

> All the concrete arguments for a late date for the Johannine literature have now been dissipated, and Bultmann's attempts to discern an earlier and later form of the Gospel have been entirely misleading, as both of his supposed reductions have similar Jewish backgrounds.[48]

The Synoptic Gospels and Acts. The main passage in the Synoptics which is considered to be flavored with Gnosticism is Matthew 11:27 along with the parallel reference in Luke 10:22. It is not necessary to interpret these verses on the basis of a Gnostic background. Indeed, Davies presents a strong argument for a Jewish background, especially relating to the Qumranian community and the Dead Sea Scrolls.[49]

There are only a few passages in Acts which are sometimes cited as reflecting Gnostic influence, namely 3:15; 5:31, and 20:29f. Schmithals, who usually has no problem locating Gnostic passages, has difficulty in pinpointing references to Gnosticism in the writings of Luke:

> Other than Mark and Matthew, no New Testament writer shows so little connection with Gnosticism as does Luke. In other words, it appears impossible to interpret the Lucan image of Paul as anti-Gnostic, as I myself at an earlier time had considered possible.[50]

The Pauline Epistles. Wilhelm Bousset sees the Pauline writings as being extremely influential upon the Gnostic movement:

> It is the form which Paul gave to Christianity that drew the Gnostic circles to it as would a magnet. It was most of all the pattern of Christianity as a one-sided religion of redemption and the connection of the redeemer myth with the figure of Jesus of Nazareth which, introduced by Paul into Christianity, exerted this great drawing power. For what was here preached as a mood, without regard to the broader consequences, in free inventive intuition, in inspired discourse of prophet and missionary, the Gnostic movement believed to be able to provide the foundation and the general background in terms of a worldview.[51]

Another viewpoint is that Paul has taken Gnostic vocabulary and recast it into distinct Christian doctrine.[52] Paul must have been knowledgeable concerning incipient forms of Gnosticism, but there is not conclusive evidence that the Apostle actually borrowed elements from the Gnostics to fashion into his epistles.

It does appear that one can find Gnosticism in nearly every part of the New Testament, especially in Paul's writings, if one lets his imagination be his guide. For example, it has generally been held that the enemies of Paul at Galatia were Judaizers, but Schmithals chooses to identify them as "Jewish Gnostics."[53]

Particularly fruitful for the pre-Christian Gnostic advocates are Paul's epistles to the Corinthians. One of the strangest of the conclusions drawn pertains to the interpretation of I Corinthians 10:16ff, which treats the observance of the Lord's Supper. Schmithals claims that the breaking of bread does not harken back to a Christian practice but rather to a Gnostic observance.[54] Even among scholars who favor a pre-Christian Gnosticism, there is difficulty in accepting the methodology of Schmithals. J. Munk is quite expressive in his critique:

> The author of this book lacks historical training. He forces his a priori opinions upon the texts with offensive boldness. . . . Schmithal's book is a striking proof of the decline of exegetic research since the 1930's.[55]

One must recognize that there are other ways to explain the problems at Corinth than by Gnosticism. Whether it be a pride for knowledge or a licentious lifestyle there need be no direct relationship to Gnosticism whatever. Nock is quite emphatic:

> The plain truth is that you could not have found anyone in Corinth to direct you to a Gnostic church: the overwhelming probability is that there was no such thing. It is at most possible that here (as certainly happened in Colosse) individual Christians came from or came into contact with esoteric Judaism.[56]

Among the Prison Epistles Colossians is often cited as dealing with Gnostic errors. J. B. Lightfoot is willing to concede that there might be Gnostic elements involved at this early date in a beginning stage, but he strongly rejects the development of an organized sect at this period of time.[57]

Several scholars, such as E. Percy, H. Hegermann, S. Lyonnet, A. Dupont, and H. Koester see no necessity in linking Gnosticism with the Epistle to the Colossians.[58] W. G. Kummel thinks that the erroneous teaching that Paul was writing against was a type of Jewish Gnosticism, which had come to be widely received.[59]

In the Pastoral Epistles there are several passages which mention false teachings, such as "myths and endless genealogies," I Timothy 1:4 (NIV); abstaining from marriage and certain foods, I Timothy 4:3 (NIV); "controversies and arguments," I Timothy 6:4; and "contradictions of what is falsely called knowledge," I Timothy 6:20 (NKJ).

Many scholars who do not accept Gnosticism in the earlier Pauline writings are willing to concede at least an elementary or incipient form of Gnosticism by the time he wrote the Pastorals. Nevertheless, it is possible that other alternatives exist. For example, G. Quispel suggests that those at Corinth as well as those in the Pastorals who opposed marriage may well have been Encratites rather than Gnostics:

> Perhaps it (Encratism) was present in Corinth, where Paul exhorts the Encratites not to give up marriage in spiritually

overrating their human frames. Certainly it is there too in the pastoral letters, where Jewish Encratites proclaim that the resurrection has already taken place and that marriage should be abolished.[60]

R. McL. Wilson observes that I Timothy 4:3, concerning those who require abstinence from marriage as well as certain foods, would indeed be applicable to some Gnostics, but he then wisely asks, "Were these Gnostics the only people to practice such ascetism?"[61]

The Epistle to the Hebrews. One viewpoint sees a Gnostic background for the Hebrews. E. Kasemann claims to have found several Gnostic concepts, namely (1) the heavenly travels of the Gnostic as the basis for the journey of God's people in seeking spiritual and final rest (3:11,18; 4:1,3,5,10ff); (2) the myth concerning the "Primal Man" is seen to be the foundation for identifying the Second Person of the Trinity as "Anthropos" (chapters 1,2); (3) the ingathering of the righteous is seen to be the basis of Christ's perfecting work wrought upon His people (2:10; 5:9; 7:19); (4) the myth regarding the Anthropos is seen as uniting with the messianic hopes of Judaism in pointing to the "heavenly high priest" in Hebrews.[62]

On the other hand, some scholars are impressed with parallels which seem to exist between the Dead Sea Scrolls and the Epistle to the Hebrews.[63] It would appear that the Qumran literature provides a better background for Hebrews than does Gnostic teachings.

The General Epistles. The Epistle of James is not usually considered to offer much that might relate to Gnosticism. H. J. Schoeps thinks that James has used various Gnostic "catchwords," but Guthrie is probably correct in suggesting that the Gnostics may well have borrowed from James.[64]

Bultmann sees two classes of men designated as "psychic" and "pneumatic" in James 3:16 (by implication at least); these, he concludes, relate to "Gnostic anthropology."[65] It is difficult to see any meaningful relationship in Bultmann's conclusion. It seems to be simply a conjecture which has no solid foundation upon which to rest.

Bultmann thinks that the enemies of righteousness mentioned in both II Peter 2:1 and Jude 8-11 were Gnostics.[435] This may well be, but Wilson has aptly responded to the last passage by stating that "idolatry and immorality in themselves" do not present conclusive proof of Gnosticism in Jude.[67]

The Epistles of John. Perhaps there is more unanimity among scholars concerning references to Gnosticism in I John than any other New Testament writing. While many would oppose Bultmann's position that I John is based upon pre-Christian Gnosticism,[68] Guthrie is doubtless correct when he states that "the letter belongs to a period when Gnosticism is certainly on the horizon, although not as yet fully developed."[69]

Since the Johannine literature is usually dated toward the close of the first century A.D., it is reasonable to assume that Gnosticism was making progress as far as organization and development were concerned. Therefore, it is not only possible, but also probable, that John was directing his attacks against some type or types of Gnosticism.

Critique and Conclusions

It has been obvious in the preceding discussions that the advocates of a pre-Christian Gnosticism have based their viewpoints upon a priori assumptions since the extant literature on Gnosticism is later than the New Testament writings. Wilson points out the fallacy of such a methodology:

> The assumption that the full development of later Gnosticism is already present in pre-Christian Gnosis obviously involves a begging of the question, a reading of first-century texts with second-century spectacles, and this amply justifies the reluctance of some scholars . . . to admit any widespread "Gnostic influence" in the formation stages of early Christianity.[70]

Nock has summed it up this way: "Certainly it is an unsound proceeding to take Manichaean and other texts, full of echoes of the

New Testament, and reconstruct from them something supposedly lying back of the New Testament."[71]

Another problem in the methodology of the scholars who hold to a pre-Christian Gnosticism is the assumption that wherever a supposed element of Gnosticism is found, it is assumed that the entire Gnostic system is assuredly wrapped up with it.[72] S. Neill exposes this weakness:

> Unfortunately, some scholars are less cautious than others; there is a tendency to suppose that when any Gnostic word or phrase occurs in any document that is available to us, the whole of the Gnostic myth must have been present in the mind of the writer whoever he may have been. Clearly, this is an assumption which is more readily made than proved.[73]

It is a rather dangerous procedure to force one's a priori assumptions upon a given New Testament passage and to conclude that whatever suppositions have been posited are to be accepted without question as being factual and completely trustworthy. Schmithals reveals his mode of interpretation when he states that "we must reconstruct the Gnosticism which stands in the background of the New Testament from the New Testament texts themselves. . . ."[74] Yamauchi declares that Bultmann assumed that John's Gospel was based upon a Gnostic system and then he reconstructed the Gnosticism by employing the Gospel as his chief resource.[75]

One can readily see the danger involved when there is an over-emphasis of the subjective at the expense of the objective. If one is intent upon finding a certain element in any given literature, it appears that he will always be able to find it if he alone is allowed to be the final authority.

When scholars use each other as sources of authority suspicion is bound to be raised as to the intellectual honesty of such pursuits. Yet this is a common mode of operation among the pre-Christian Gnostic scholars.[76]

Apparently some have assumed that if Gnosticism were non-Christian it must also be pre-Christian, but Quispel has stated it thus:

"It is becoming increasingly clear that Gnosis in its essential being is non-Christian; the view that it is also pre-Christian must still be proven."[77] In light of the late dates for Gnostic literature it seems best to date Gnosticism sometime after the institution of Christianity. Drivers expresses the matter as follows:

> We can reduce this whole complex of relations to two questions; was there a pre-Christian Gnosticism, and were there forms of Gnosticism that are non-Christian? For non-Christian does not automatically mean pre-Christian. In spite of all the suppositions in this field, we know nothing of a pre-Christian Gnostic system.[78]

See Appendix E for an assessment on pre-Christian Gnosticism.

The remaining four chapters will discuss various ways whereby man obtains knowledge of God.

Chapter Two

KNOWLEDGE BY NATURE

A number of New Testament passages indicate that God has not left Himself without witness to all men. W. B. Godbey notes that God has so manifested Himself unconditionally to all of mankind by three means, namely "the Holy Spirit, the light of nature, and human conscience."[79]

The manifestation of Himself which God makes to the entire human family is variously termed by scholars, such as (1) Natural Revelation, (2) General Revelation, or (3) External Revelation.[80] In contrast to this type of revelation is the manifestation of God in the Person and work of Christ , which is sometimes designated as (1) Special Revelation, (2) Supernatural Revelation, or (3) Internal Revelation.[81]

In this chapter special attention will be directed to several New Testament passages which indicate that God has in fact disclosed some things about Himself to all men.

Romans 1:18-23

When Paul wrote his epistle to the Romans, it appears that he had not yet had the privilege of making a personal visit to Rome (1:13; 15:22-24). Perhaps this explains, in part at least, the extensive detail given in various doctrinal discussions.

At any rate, one of the most important passages which treats God's revelation of Himself to all men is found in the first chapter of Romans. After his usually long introduction Paul comes to the very heart, the central motif of his letter in chapter one, verses 16 and 17. Herein he declares that the good news of Christ pertains to a sufficient salvation provided for all men which is conditioned on faith.

Following the announcement of his theme Paul then states that "the wrath of God is revealed from heaven against all ungodliness and unrighteousness of men, who hold the truth in unrighteousness" (1:18, KJV).

Verse nineteen opens with "διότι" (dee-ot-ee, because), which apparently introduces the reason for the revelation of God's wrath: it is simply because God has already disclosed enough knowledge about Himself to hold men accountable. It may also be that verse 19 is supporting the participial phrase in the latter part of verse 18 by expressing the fact that men have received enough knowledge of truth that they turn against it and suppress it.[82]

Two positions have been taken concerning the meaning of "τὸ γνωστὸν τοῦ θεοῦ" (to gnoston tou theou); (1) H. A. W. Meyer claims that the phrase means "that which is known concerning God";[83] C. E. B. Cranfield declares that it means "that which is knowable (to man) of God."[84] James Denney states that it is impossible to determine whether "γνωστόν" in this passage means "known" or "knowable," but he correctly concludes that "what is meant in either case is the knowledge of God which is independent of such a special revelation as had been given to the Jews."[85]

Perhaps both meanings are intended since all men must receive at least a certain degree of knowledge concerning God and truth in order to be held accountable. On the other hand, it does appear that one could become more knowledgeable by giving a proper response of obedient acceptance to the knowledge already received.

In verse 20 Paul points to God's method of revelation: He reveals His own invisible characteristics by means of the created universe. Willard H. Taylor says that this visible created world does reveal "some raw materials of the knowledge of God."[86] Two things are revealed about God by means of the created universe, namely (1) His omnipotence, which is reflected in the design, beauty, order and laws of the universe; and (2) His divine nature. Since the cause must always be greater than the effect, it is reasonable to conclude that the Creator must be divine. It is because of these revelations that Paul goes on to say that "men are without excuse." The phrase "εἰς τὸ εἶναι" (eis to einai) expresses either purpose[87] or result.[88]

Verse 21 explicitly states that the heathen "knew God." Yet in Galatians 4:8 and I Thessalonians 4:5 Paul clearly asserts that they do not know God. Obviously there is a particular sense in which they knew God, but another sense in which they did not know Him.

Certainly they knew God as the all-powerful Creator and Preserver of the universe, yet they knew Him not as Sovereign Lord and Savior. Having been the recipients of the initial knowledge of God and truth they refused to glorify, honor, esteem or worship God by submitting to His authority. Furthermore, they refused to show appreciation to God by their failure to offer thanksgiving to Him for blessings received.

Verses 21 and 22 record three consequences: (1) "their thinking became futile;" (2) "their foolish hearts were darkened;" and (3) "they became fools" (NIV used for each reference). All this led to idolatry (v. 23). James A. Stifler wisely notes that "the refusal to accept the truth destroys the power to discriminate between truth and error."[89]

Romans 2:12-16

A second important passage which treats general or natural revelation is found in the second chapter of Romans. It will be observed that verse 14 refers to nature (φύσει, phusei) which in effect becomes a teacher in itself. The Apostle Paul also refers to the influence of nature in I Corinthians 11:14 (NKJ): "Does not even nature itself teach you. . . ."

In the opening verses of chapter two Paul points out three principles which God employs in his judgment upon men: His judgment is (1) "according to truth," v. 2; "according to one's deeds," v. 6; and (3) without "respect of persons," v. 11. Hence, there is no superiority of the Jew.

The chief difference between Jew and Gentile does not pertain to race but to revelation.[90] The Jews have received the written revelation of God in the Law or the Torah. The Gentiles were not recipients of the written law. Yet the Gentile heathen were still capable of committing sin even though they did not possess the written law of the Jews. On what basis could God hold them responsible? Verse 14 reveals the answer: "for when Gentiles, who do not have the law, by nature do the things contained in the law, these, although not having the law, are a law to themselves (NKJ).

In explaining the meaning of the expression "by nature" J. A. Beet states that it means "the outworking of forces born in us, as distinguished from results of education and later events."[91]   Whedon identifies "nature" as "natural conscience" and yet he claims that even among pagans "nature is not alone or unaided."[92]   It does seem best to attribute any ability of heathen to do what is enjoined by Law, not simply to native powers or abilities, but to the grace of God. John Wesley would attribute it to the prevenient grace of God which is bestowed on all men:

> Allowing that all the souls of men are dead in sin by nature, this excuses none, seeing there is no man that is in a state of mere nature; there is no man, unless he has quenched the Spirit, that is wholly void of the grace of God. No man living is entirely destitute of what is vulgarly called "natural conscience." But this is not natural: it is more properly termed "preventing grace." Every man has a greater or less measure of this, which waiteth not for the call of man. Every one has, sooner or later, good desires; although the generality of men stifle them before they can strike deep root, or produce any considerable fruit. Every one has some measure of that light, some faint glimmering ray, which, sooner or later, more or less, enlightens every man that cometh into the world. . . . So that no man sins because he has not grace, but because he does not use the grace which he hath.[93]

Verse 15 indicates that when heathen do what the Law requires, without having the written Law, they reveal "the work of the law written in their hearts" (KJV). Stifler points out that Paul does not say that the law itself is written upon the heart, but only its work, which he illustrates as follows: "A machine may show the work of intelligence, but it has none."[94]

Whedon thinks that τò ἔργον τοῦ νομου (to ergon tou nomou) may either mean "the practice which the law enjoins, or the operation of the law," but he prefers the latter.[95]   Barrett suggests that it means "the effect of the law," and goes on to state that the law has "left its stamp upon their minds;" this stamp he identifies as man's conscience.[96] On the other hand, Cranfield disagrees with Barrett and asserts that the expression means "the work which the law requires . . . in the sense of the prescription contained in the law."[97]

Whatever the precise meaning may be, one can at least safely conclude that God has etched upon the minds of all men, especially those who have never been privileged to possess a Bible, an unwritten law, which, if obeyed, would have the same end result as for a Jew who has obeyed the written revelation. Does this mean that one could be saved without having the written Word of God? Could heathen people be converted simply by obeying the light which they have received? Scholars vary in their interpretation of the passages cited above in Romans. S. Lewis Johnson cites three sources from which man obtains a knowledge of God, as related in Romans chapter two, namely (1) nature, (2) conscience, and (3) the Bible; but the first two, he claims are not sufficient to bring one into salvation.[98] In contrast to such a viewpoint is that of W. B. Godbey, who declares that the heathen possess knowledge of God by means of the Holy Spirit, conscience, and nature, which provide sufficient knowledge for one's salvation if one will simply walk in the light so shed upon his path.[99] Yet Godbey recognizes that these three sources of light are often dimmed by the subtle attacks of Satan.[100]

See Appendix F for an interesting account of an old Indian chief who Godbey claims was truly saved without the possession of a Bible.

It does seem that Godbey's position best fits the total teaching of the New Testament. If one cannot possibly be saved without the written revelation of God, how can it be said that "there is no respect of persons with God" (Romans 2:11, KJV)? Is it the fault of heathen that they have not received the Word of God? If indeed the full responsibility of the salvation of pagans depends upon the outreach of missionaries, what happens if men fail to fulfill their obligations? Will pagans be lost because men have failed? If so, one must conclude that throughout history multitudes of mankind have never really had a chance to be saved. It would appear that under such a system they were predestined to be lost. This viewpoint simply does not square with New Testament teaching which emphatically states that the Lord "is not willing that any should perish, but that all should come to repentance" (II Peter 3:9, KJV).

John 1:9

The Apostle John adds further content to the Pauline statements concerning the natural or general revelation of God to all men. John identifies the Logos as "the true light that gives light to every man" (John 1:9, NIV). Marcus Dods points out that the expression τὸ φῶς τὸ ἀληθινόν (to phos to alethinos) is used nine times by John, but never by the Synoptic writers.[101]

Wesley relates this light to man's "natural conscience" and claims that if man would not resist this light, it "would shine more and more to the perfect day."[102] Apparently Wesley's position is virtually the same as that taken by Godbey, namely that a man could be finally saved even if he never had a Bible nor heard a Gospel message on the basis that he did not rebel against the light shed upon his conscience.

Calvin likewise declares that this true light shines upon the conscience of every man.[103] He also notes that this inshining light bestows upon man a rational faculty which distinguishes him from the lower animals.[104]

It is of interest to note that the Quakers have used this verse to teach that God visits all men with grace so that no one is denied a time of divine visitation.[105] The Quaker theologian, Barclay, referred to the verse as follows: "This place doth so clearly favor us that by some it is called 'the Quaker's text,' for it doth evidently demonstrate our assertion."[106]

The universal dissemination of the light of Christ to all men is an additional testimony to the fact that He is no respecter of persons. Is it not reasonable to assume that this light is given to every man for the purpose of leading each one into the light of a knowledge of sins forgiven?

Westcott correctly concludes that "no man is wholly destitute of the illumination of 'the Light.' In nature, and life, and conscience it makes itself felt in various degrees to all."[107]

Acts 10:34-35

Various passages might yet be cited in support of natural or general revelation, but only one more will be discussed in this chapter. The context reveals that Peter was still plagued with prejudice, with an erroneous idea that Jews were superior to Gentiles until the Lord was able to correct his thinking by means of a vision and a rebuke.

By the time he arrived at the home of Cornelius in Caesarea, Peter was thoroughly convinced that God did not have favorites among mankind. He was so certain that God is not partial in His love to any one that he declared, "In truth I perceive that God shows no partiality" (Acts 10:34, NKJ). Only God could have persuaded Peter of that fact.

Verse 35 unfolds a specific manner in which God discloses His impartiality; He "accepts men from every nation who fear Him and do right" (NIV). Does this mean that a heathen who does not have a Bible and has never heard a Gospel message could indeed find acceptance with God in spite of those omissions if he walks in what little light he has received through nature and his conscience?

There is a diversity of opinion among the scholars. For example, Ramsay interprets the verse to mean that Cornelius was a proselyte to Judaism and on that basis accepted into Christianity.[108] This is only a conjecture and one that is not satisfactory because it lacks solid evidence.

Verse 35 clearly states that a man's nationality is not an important factor with God, but the way he responds to the knowledge of God which he has received is most important. Meyer claims that the statement "acceptable to Him" means "to be received into the Christian fellowship with God."[109]

Wesley understands the verse to mean that if a man has reverence for God and does all he knows to be right in accordance with the light he has received, he will be "accepted of Him," but the acceptance is "through Christ, though he knows Him not."[110] Wesley affirms that no one can be acceptable to God except through Christ Who alone has provided redemption. Because Christ has died for all men, the atonement is universal; God can therefore accept a man who fears Him and works righteousness to the best of his ability. However, there is a greater blessing to be received as Wesley clearly notes:

He is in the favor of God, whether enjoying His written word and ordinances or not. Nevertheless the addition of these is an unspeakable blessing to those who were before in some measure accepted. Otherwise God would never have sent an angel from heaven to direct Cornelius to St. Peter.[111]

G. Campbell Morgan claims that a heathen man can be saved, not because he understands the atonement, but because he fears God and works righteousness, which is not based on the merits of his moral works, but on the merits of the cross of Christ.[112]

Perhaps the clearest discussion on the above passage is that given by Dr. Whedon who endeavors to effect a balanced interpretation that fits into the total teaching of the New Testament:

> In heathen lands this will appear in rectitude of life. In Christian lands it will appear in faith in Christ and obedience to his holy requirements. The unbelieving moralist who quotes this text to prove his acceptability with God shows by the very fact of his unbelief that he does not truly fear God. That Cornelius feared God and was a devout man truly appears from the fact that from the very moment Christ was announced to him he accepted Christ. And so there may be thousands who never heard of Christ, who have that spirit of faith which would heartily accept him were he truly known to them.[113]

In light of the above scriptures one may conclude that God has shed upon the minds of all men a measure of light that imparts sufficient knowledge to know there is a God and that there is a difference between right and wrong. Therefore no one will be able to plead ignorance in the day of judgment. Adam Clarke declares that "no man can be accepted with this just God who does not live up to the advantages of the state in which providence has placed him."[114]

Chapter Three

KNOWLEDGE BY THE WORD OF GOD

God has manifested Himself to the entire populace of mankind through His created universe but that manifestation has of necessity been limited to His power and divine nature. With the entrance of sin into the human family a special revelation was needed in order to disclose God's plan of redemption. It has been suggested that something more than natural revelation is required "because divine tuition must contend against the abnormal consequences of sin as discerned in the apathy, perversity and spiritual darkness which characterize the minds of men."[115]

If man is to know the mind of God in regard to both sin and salvation, there must be a revelation given by God which would make known what nature could never disclose. Such a revelation was given in a written propositional form known as the sacred scriptures. Without a knowledge of God's Word man would always be in the dark concerning his origin, purpose upon the earth, and final destiny. The scripture paints man's picture just as it is, and shows him not only his sinful condition but a Savior who can save him from his sins.

In the scriptures are found "a more sure word of prophecy" (II Peter 1:19, KJV). It is identified as an "incorruptible seed" which is actively involved in the new birth (I Peter 1:23, KJV). It is called "the word of truth" (James 1:18, KJV). Jesus said, "Search the scriptures; for in them ye think ye have eternal life: and they are they which testify of me" (John 5:39, KJV).

The revelation of God through the created world does not contradict that of the scripture; rather each complements and supplements the other. The interrelations between the two have been aptly expressed thus:

> The Earth and the Bible are God's two texts, each having its place, time and function in progressive revelation. Nature is the primary source of knowledge, the Bible is the supplementary

source. Nature proposes mysterious questions, and the Bible in so far as it is understood solves them. The Bible furnishes us with ideals, Nature gives us the tools with which to work them out. The one tells us of His eternal power and Godhead, the other of His mercy and love. Without the Bible the universe would be a riddle; without Nature, the Bible would be meaningless.[116]

The importance of the Word of God in relation to a proper knowledge of God is vividly stated in the Johannine literature. In his Gospel he wrote: "these are written, that ye might believe that Jesus is the Christ, the Son of God; and that believing ye might have life through his name" (John 20:32, KJV). In his First Epistle John expressed it this way: "These things have I written unto you that believe on the name of the Son of God; that ye may know that ye have eternal life, and that ye may believe on the name of the Son of God" (I John 5:13, KJV). John also adds that "we can be sure we know him if we obey his commands" (I John 2:3, NIV).

Chapter Four

KNOWLEDGE THROUGH CHRIST

The greatest revelation of God is seen in the Person of Jesus Christ, for "the Son is the radiance of God's glory and the exact representation of His being" (Hebrews 1:3a,b, NIV). When Philip asked Jesus to show the disciples the Father, He responded, "He that hath seen Me hath seen the Father" (John 14:9, KJV).

John 1:14

Josh McDowell suggests that, if God had wanted to communicate with man, the best way He could directly do so would be to become a man.[117] If God were then to become a man, among other things one would expect that He would "have an unusual entrance into life."[118] This transpired in the virgin birth which had been foretold by Isaiah nearly seven centuries before the occurrence. Certainly this "unusual entrance" goes beyond man's ability to comprehend. Paul acknowledges that "the mystery of godliness is great" and then states, "He appeared in a body" (I Timothy 3:16, NIV). John declares that "the Word was made flesh and dwelt among us (and we beheld his glory, the glory as of the only begotten of the Father) full of grace and truth" (John 1:14, KJV).

Matthew 11:27

No doubt the most important passage in the Synoptics on man's knowledge of God is found in Matthew 11:27, "No man knoweth the Son, but the Father; neither knoweth any man the Father, save the Son and he to whomsoever the Son will reveal him" (KJV). This passage has been called "a Johannine thunderbolt in the synoptic sky."[119] Alan Richardson states that this verse is so important that all the remaining New Testament verses upon this subject can be considered as a commentary on it.[120]

It is obvious that only an infinite mind can understand an infinite Person; therefore it is not strange that the Members of the Godhead alone understand and know each other fully. Yet Christ is authorized to reveal the Father to whomsoever He chooses.

Verse 25 reveals that the Father has hidden spiritual knowledge from those who consider themselves "wise and learned" but has disclosed it to those who are identified as "babes" or "little children." Apparently the "wise and learned" were those who were too proud to repent and submit to the Lordship of Christ, whereas the "little children" were those who gladly accepted the Gospel and yielded themselves to it. The end result is always dependent upon the response of man. Whedon asserts that "the wise and prudent may, if they choose, become the babes. And then they will cease to be those from whom the Gospel is hid."[121] Verse 28 extends an invitation to all the weary to come to Christ and take His yoke upon them that they might learn true knowledge.

John 1:18

Another passage demands brief attention, namely John 1:18 which reads as follows: "No one has seen God at any time. The only begotten Son, who is in the bosom of the Father, He has declared Him" (NKJ). Verse 17 declares that Christ brought both grace and truth. As Westcott sees it, "truth" which denotes reality is synonymous with "the knowledge of God."[122] Westcott has summed up verse 18 with uncommon insight:

> This last verse justifies the claim of the Gospel to be the Truth, while it lays down the inherent limitations of human knowledge. It is impossible, so far as our experience yet goes, for man to have direct knowledge of God as God. He can come to know Him only through One who shares both the human and divine natures, and who is in vital fellowship both with God and with man. In Christ this condition is satisfied. He who as the Word has been declared to be God, who as the Son is one in essence with the Father, even He set forth that which we need to know. It is tacitly assumed throughout, as it will be

observed, that "the Truth" and "the knowledge of God" are identical terms.[123]

Thus one observes that Christ the Son makes known the Unknowable and at the same time makes visible the Invisible.[124] In his Epistle to the Colossians Paul affirms the fact that Christ is "the image of the invisible God" and furthermore he announces that "it pleased the Father that in Him all the fullness should dwell" (Colossians 1:15,19, NKJ). Those who have received Christ have been the recipients of "the light of the knowledge of the glory of God in the face of Jesus Christ" (II Corinthians 4:6, KJV).

Chapter Five

KNOWLEDGE THROUGH THE HOLY SPIRIT

Jesus came into the world to reveal His heavenly Father, lay down His life as a ransom for lost humanity, arise from the dead and ascend to the right hand of the Father where He continually makes intercession. How it saddened the hearts of His disciples to learn that He must go to Jerusalem where He would suffer many things of the Jews and finally be crucified. However, Jesus assured His followers that He would not leave them comfortless, but would send unto them the Comforter Who is the Holy Spirit. He is further identified as "the Spirit of Truth" Who Jesus said would take the things of His (Christ's) and show them to His disciples.

I Corinthians 2:9-12

In I Corinthians chapter 2 Paul speaks about two classifications of men, namely the natural and the spiritual. The natural man is the one who is taken up with the spirit and wisdom of this world. His spiritual nature or capacity has been deadened by the effects of sin so that He is unable to receive the things of the Holy Spirit," neither can he know them, because they are spiritually discerned" (I Corinthians 2:14, KJV).

Although the spiritual realities of the Kingdom of God are hidden from the natural man, "God hath revealed them to us by his Spirit" (I Corinthians 2:10, KJV). Only the Holy Spirit can take the things of the Father and the Son and make them known to man, for "nothing but omniscience can know omniscience."[125]

I John 3:24; 4:13; 5:10

One of the most important New Testament doctrines relating to soteriology that has often been neglected pertains to the assurance of salvation. Yet the Scripture is clear and emphatic.

In John's First Epistle he records various ways one can know certain facts. In the physical realm one knows certain things by means of one's physical senses, 1:1. In the spiritual realm one knows he is in right relationship with God because (1) he keeps God's commandments, 2:3,5; (2) he lives an upright life, 2:29; (3) he loves God's people, 3:14; (4) he has the abiding presence of the Holy Spirit with him, 3:24; 4:13; 5:10.

The sweetest assurance possible to a child of God is that testimony which God Himself gives by the indwelling presence of the Holy Spirit. This witness is internal and is obtained by faith, according to I John 5:10.

Galatians 4:6-7

Galatians 4:5 sums up the purpose for which Christ came into the world: "to redeem those who were under the law, that we might receive the adoption as sons" (NKJ). Christ came to deliver men from the shackles of sin. The contrast between "slave" and "son" in verse 7 should be carefully noted. The former is characterized by bondage and burden, whereas the latter is known for his liberty and privileges.

To certify one's sonship the Father sends the Holy Spirit into one's heart, bearing witness to the reality of the fact. The Spirit cries out, "Abba, Father," which is "the filial cry, from a loving son, upon the recognition of a loving Father."[126]

Martin Luther saw the need for emphasis upon this important doctrine in light of the neglect and omission in the Roman Catholic Church:

> The Roman theologians teach that no man can know for a certainty whether he stands in the favor of God or not. This teaching forms one of the chief articles of their faith. With this teaching they tormented men's consciences, excommunicated Christ from the Church, and limited the operations of the Holy Ghost.[127]

Romans 8:15-16

Verse 15 is a parallel passage to Galatians 4:6,7. However, verse 16 of Romans 8 is considered the classic New Testament verse treating the witness of the Holy Spirit to one's sonship.

Denney calls attention to punctuation in Westcott and Hort which renders verse 16: "in that we cry, Abba, Father, the Spirit itself beareth witness with our spirit."[128] He further observes that "our own spirit tells us we are God's children, but the voice with which it speaks is, as we know, prompted and inspired by the Divine Spirit itself."[129]

Beet notes that the term "witness" is one that the Greeks were fond of using whenever they wanted to establish a proof.[130] Thus Paul is stating that the evidence is established for one's filial relationship with God when the Spirit bears witness with one's own spirit. The verb συμμαρτυρέω (summartureo) denotes a two-fold witness, that of God's Spirit and also man's spirit.

This joint relationship should also be viewed in regard to the cry that is made at the time the Spirit bears witness. According to Ramm:

> The locus of the "testimonium" is the human spirit, and both the divine Spirit and the human spirit cry the same thing, "Father." These are not two cries but one cry. They are like two forks of the same pitch which vibrate sympathetically and harmoniously together. We both cry; we both cry "Father"—it is the same cry, the same content, to the same God.[131]

It would then appear that the energizing activity of the Spirit precipitates in man's spirit a harmonious cry at the point of reconciliation. Ramm states that "we cry 'Father' because it indicates that our redemption and adoption is accomplished."[132]

Although Scripture does relate certain characteristics about the witness of the Spirit to one's sonship, there is no explicit definition given in the Word. Indeed it is not an easy task to define the witness. One of the clearest articulations as to the meanings of the witness is expressed by Wesley as follows:

> The testimony of the Spirit is an inward impression on the soul, whereby the Spirit of God directly witnesses to my spirit, that I am a child of God; that Jesus Christ hath loved me, and given himself for me; and that all my sins are blotted out, and I, even I, am reconciled to God.[133]

It should be emphasized that a balance must be maintained between the emotions and the intellect. The Holy Spirit always functions in alignment with the Word of God. This balance must always be kept in order to steer one away from the dangers of fanaticism.

Before concluding this chapter, there needs to be some mention of the matter of personal responsibility. God does not arbitrarily choose one to come to the knowledge of sonship apart from human cooperation. John 7:17 (KJV) sums it up tersely: "If any man will do his will, he shall know of the doctrine." Man must first know God's will, and this involves his intellect; he must then choose to obey God's commands which entails his will power; the end result is the obtaining of knowledge which brings joy and peace, thus touching one's emotions. It is God's will that all men come to know Him as Sovereign Lord and Savior.

CONCLUSION

Man has always sought to know ultimate truth, to know God. The methods of search have varied, the end results have been different, but the common denominator of an inward aspiration to know the Ultimate Being of the universe has crossed every racial and cultural boundary. Something has been placed in man, indeed a light from the Creator, which causes man to be restless unless he come to a knowledge of God.

Left to his imagination and emotions man has manufactured strange ideas about God that are always reflected in his mode of life, his ethical standards. In His unfolding providence God has provided an objective revelation in the form of written, propositional Scripture to point man to the source of help in order to satisfy the subjective longings of his heart.

In light of the above research the following conclusions may be drawn: (1) man cannot know himself except as God makes a revelation to him by the mirror of the Bible and the ministry of the Holy Spirit; (2) God is faithful to reveal to an awakened person the solution to his sin problem in the Gospel of Jesus Christ; (3) by grace the penitent believer is enabled to repent and believe the Gospel; (4) the impartation of God's saving grace is certified to the believer by the witness of the Holy Spirit and also by the witness of his own spirit; (5) such a recipient of divine grace then *knows* he is a son of God, and cries, "Abba, Father."

Of course there is much room to expand one's knowledge of the will and way of God throughout life so that one may prepare to be with Christ forever and ever. Paul expressed his testimony this way: "I know whom I have believed, and am persuaded that He is able to keep that which I have committed unto Him against that day" II Timothy 1:12, KJV).

APPENDIX A

The following comments on three Greek synonyms are taken from *Some Lessons of the Revised Version of the New Testament* (New York: James Pott and Co., 1897), 100-103, B. F. Westcott.

It was far more easy to suggest to the English reader the shades of thought represented by the different Greek words answering to "*to be*" than of those answering to "*to know*." Three words clearly distinct in conception (εἰδέναι, γινώσκειν, ἐπίστασθαι) are commonly, and for the most part necessarily to be translated. Of these, two are very common (εἰδέναι, γινώσκειν), one of which (εἰδέναι) describes, so to speak, a direct mental vision, knowledge which is at once immediate and complete; and the other (γινώσκειν) a knowledge which moves from point to pint, springing out of observation and experience. The third word (ἐπίστασθαι) is much rarer, and expresses the knowledge which comes from close and familiar acquaintance. It will be evident that in many cases nothing but a paraphrase could convey the precise meaning of the original. Elsewhere the context gives the appropriate colour to the general term (*know*). In some places, however, it seemed desirable to mark the contrast when two of the words were placed in close connection. Thus in John iii.10,11 there is a contrast between the absolute knowledge of the Lord and that power of recognizing truth which an accredited master might be expected to possess; and thus the Revised Version gives, in strict conformity with the Greek, *Art thou the teacher of Israel, and understandest* (Authorised Version, knowest) *not these things?* Verily, verily, I say unto thee, We speak that we do know . . . . So again we see a little more of the meaning of the words by which the Lord replies to the impetuous question with which St. Peter met His offer of lowly service, when we read in the Revised Version, *What I do thou knowest not now; but thou shalt understand* (Authorised Version, know) *hereafter,* taught in the solemn school of apostolic work (John xiii.7). In one or two places the substitution of *learn* for *know* (γινώσκειν) adds to the narrative the touch of life which belongs to the progress of events; as when it is said, on the eve of the triumphal entry in Jerusalem, that *the common people of the Jews* learned (Authorised Version, knew) *that [Jesus] was [at Bethany]* . . . (John xii.9). The phrase suggests the idea of lively interest and inquiry, which prepare for what followed. There is a similar vividness in the use of *perceive; the disciples perceived* (Authorised Version, knew) *not the things that were said when the Lord spoke of His passion* (Luke XVIII.34); they could not read the signs before them. The use of this word (perceive) of the Lord emphasises a trait in His perfect humanity. Looking on the anxious faces of the disciples He perceived (Authorized Version, knew) *that they were desirous to ask Him* . . . (John xvi. 19).

APPENDIX B

Donald W. Burdick gives the following classification of Paul's usages of οἶδα and γινώσκω in a chapter entitled "Οἶδα and Γινώσκω in the Pauline Epistles" in *New Dimensions in New Testament Study*, ed. R. N. Longenecker and M. C. Tenney (Grand Rapids: Zondervan Publishing House, 1974), 355,356.

I. Passages where οἶδα is used in its classical sense (90 passages):

Rom.	2:2	13:2	Col. 3:24
	3:19	14:11	4:1
	5:3	14:16	4:6
	6:9	15:58	I Thess. 1:4
	6:16	16:15	1:5
	7:14	2 Cor. 1:7	2:1
	8:22	4:14	2:2
	8:27	5:1	2:5
	8:28	5:6	2:11
	11:2	5:16a	3:3
	14:14	11:11	3:4
	15:29	11:31	4:2
I Cor.	1:16	12:2a	4:4
	2:2	12:2b	4:5
	2:11a	12:2c	5:2
	3:16	12:2d	2 Thess. 1:8
	5:6	12:3a	2:6
	6:2	12:3b	3:7
	6:3	12:3c	I Tim. 1:8
	6:9	Gal. 2:16	1:9
	6:15	4:8	3:5
	6:16	4:13	3:15
	6:19	Eph. 5:5	2 Tim. 1:12

7:16a	6:8	2:23
7:16b	6:9	3:14
8:1	Phil. 1:16	3:15
8:4	1:19	Titus 1:16
9:13	1:25	3:11
9:24	4:12a	Philem 21
12:2	4:15	

II. Passages where the sense of οἶδα is equivocal (5 usages):

Rom. 8:26   2 Cor. 5:11   2 Tim. 1:15
     13:11   9:2

III. Passages where οἶδα has the meaning of classical γινώσκω (8 usages):

Rom. 7:7b   11:3   Col. 2:1
     7:18   Eph. 1:18   I Thess. 5:12
I Cor. 2:12   6:21

IV. Passages where γινώσκω is used in its classical sense (32 usages):

Rom.	2:18		13:12		4:9b
	7:7a		14:7	Eph.	3:19
	11:34		14:9		6:22
I Cor.	1:21	2 Cor.	2:4	Phil.	1:12
	2:14		2:9		2:19
	2:16		3:2		3:10
	4:19		5:21		4:5
	8:2a		13:6	Col.	4:8
	8:2b	Gal.	2:9	I Thess.	3:5
	8:2c		3:7	2 Tim.	3:1
	13:9		4:9a		

V. Passages where the sense of γινώσκω is equivocal (8 usages):

Rom.	1:21		10:19	2 Cor.	8:9
	3:17	I Cor.	2:8a	Phil.	2:22
	7:15		2:8b		

VI. Passages where γινώσκω has the meaning of classical οἶδα (10 usages):

Rom.	6:6		8:3	2 Tim.	1:18
	7:1	2 Cor.	5:16b		2:19
	2:11b		5:16c		
I Cor.	3:20	Eph.	5:5		

APPENDIX C

The following comments and chart are taken from a chapter entitled "The Pauline Style as Lexical Choice: ΓΙΝΩΣΚΕΙΝ and Related Verbs" in *Pauline Studies*, ed. D. A. Hagner and M. J. Harris (The Paternoster Press LTD, 1980), 188-96.

Two notations have been used to accompany the references, an asterisk and a question mark, both of which advise the reader to examine the passage so marked. The asterisk calls attention to the fact that the context—including one whole verse preceding and following the reference—contains data that may be useful or even necessary before drawing inferences. Most of these asterisked passages contain closely related terms which may have affected the use of the verb under consideration.

The question mark, on the other hand, alerts the user to the possibility that the reference does not really belong where it is listed. For example, it may be that the syntagmatic combination can be interpreted in more than one way; in such cases, the references have been usually listed under more than one heading (e.g. when the verb both rules a direct object and is followed by ὅΤΙ). Again, it may be that the particular occurrence of the verb suggests a meaning too far from "to know." And so on. It seemed best to err on the side of fullness of information, since the user would find it easier to omit consideration of a verse than to search out what he is interested in verifying.

For similar reasons, all of the epistles which bear Paul's name have been included. The references are listed according to their order in the New Testament; scholars who wish to exclude the material from any epistle for whatever reason can do so without difficulty. Finally, many cross-references of various types have been included to make the lists as serviceable as possible.

The Semantic Field "To Know" in Paul

I. Ruling a Direct Object

NOTE: Included here, in addition to the obvious references, are (a) passages where the verb is ruling a relative clause and (b) examples of apparent absolute uses where the object is explicit in the immediate context (cf. τὰ τοῦ πνεύματος γνῶναι in 2 Cor. 2:14; some of the decisions may be debatable).

ἀγνοεῖν
    Rom. 10:3*; 11:25 (+ ὅτι)
    I Cor. 14:38* a, b (variant reading)
    2 Cor. 2:11*

ἀκούειν
    Rom. 10:14a (cf verses 18f.)
    I Cor. 2:9* (Isa. 64:4); 14:2?
    Gal. 1:13; 4:21
    Eph. 1:13,15; 3:2*; 4:21*
    Phil. 1:27,30*; 4:9*
    Col. 1:4, (5 προακούειν), 6*, 9*, 23
    2 Thess. 3:11 (acc. ptc. = ind. Discourse)
    2 Tim. 1:13*; 2:2; 4:17?
    Phlm. 5

ἀνακρίνειν
    I Cor. 2:15*; 4:3*, 4*

ἀρνεῖσθαι ?
    Titus 1:16* (opp. ὁμολογοῦσιν εἰδέναι)

αὐγάζειν
    2 Cor. 4:4*

ἀφιδεῖν
    Phil. 2:23* (nuance "find out")

βλέπειν
    Rom. 7:23* (cf. verse 21)
    I Cor. 1:26? (+ὅτι); 10:18 ?
    II Cor. 10:7*
    Col. 2:5; 4:17 ?

γινώσκειν
    Rom. 1:21*; 3:17 (Isa. 59:8); 6:6 (+ ὅτι); 7:1*, 7*, 15*; 11:34* (Isa.
    40:13)

    I Cor. 2:8* a, b, 11*, 14*, 16* (Isa. 40:13; 3:20* (+ ὅΤΙ; Ps. 94:11);
    4:19; 8:2*a

2 Cor. 5:16*a, b,21; 8:9 (+ ὅτι)
Gal. 2:9 (cf. verse 7); 4:9*
Eph. 3:19*
Phil. 2:22*; 3:10
2 Tim. 1:18; 2:19 (Num. 16:5); 3:1 (+ ὅτι)

ἔγραψα + ἵνα γνῶ(τε) + dir. obj., or analogous construction (= "find out")

2 Cor. 2:4*, 9
Eph. 6:22*
Phil. 2:19? (cf. construction in verse 28)
Col. 4:8*
1 Thess. 3:5*

δέχεσθαι?
1 Cor. 2:14* (cf. 2 Cor. 6:1; 1 Thess. 1:6*; 2:13; 2 Thess. 2:10)

διακρίνειν?
1 Cor. 4:7*; 11:29*, 31

δοκιμάζειν
Rom. 2:18*; 14:22*?
1 Cor. 11:28*
2 Cor. 13:5* Phil. 1:10*
1 Thess. 2:4* b

εἰδέναι
Rom. 7:7*; 8:26?; 13:11 (+ ὅτι)
1 Cor. 2:2, 11*, 12*; 13:2*; 14:11; 16:15 (+ ὅτι)
2 Cor. 5:16*; 9:2; 12:2* a, 3* a (+ ὅτι, verse 4)
Gal. 4:8*
Eph. 5:5* (+ ὅτι?); 6:21* (nuance "find out")
1 Thess. 1:4 (+ ὅτι, verse 5?); 2:1* (+ ὅτι); 4:5*; 5:12*
2 Thess. 1:8*; 2:6*
1 Tim. 1:9* (+ ὅτι)
2 Tim. 1:12*, 15 (+ ὅτι)
Titus 1:16*

ἐπιγινώσκειν
Rom. 1:32 (+ ὅτι)

I Cor. 14:37* (+ ὅτι); 16:18?
2 Cor. 1:13* a, 14* (+ ὅτι ?); 13:5* (+ ὅτι)
Col. 1:6*
I Tim. 4:3

ἐπίστασθαι
    I Tim. 6:4*

ἐραυνᾶν
    Rom. 8:27*
    I Cor. 2:10*

εὑρίσκειν
    Rom. 7:21 (cf. verse 23)
    2 Cor. 9:4; 12:20a

ἰδεῖν
    Rom. 11:22
    I Cor. 2:9* (Isa. 64:4)
    Phil. 1:30*; 4:9*

καταλαμβάνειν
    Phil. 3:12a, 13 (cf. Gal. 4:8f.)

καταλαμβάνεσθαι
    Eph. 3:18*

κατανοεῖν
    Rom. 4:19

κρίνειν ?
    2 Cor. 5:14 (+ ὅτι)

μανθάνειν
    I Cor. 4:6*
    Gal. 3:2*
    Eph. 4:20*
    Phil. 4:9
    Col. 1:7*
    2 Tim. 3:14a,b

μιμνήσκεσθαι
2 Tim. I:4 (cf. εἰδὼς ὅτι)

μνημονεύειν
I Thess. I:3*; 2:9*

νοεῖν
Eph. 3:4* (nuance "find out"; προέγραψα, verse 3), 20*
I Tim. I:7*
2 Tim. 2:7?

παρακολουθεῖν
I Tim. 4:6
2 Tim. 3:10*

παραλαμβάνεσθαι?
Phil. 4:9* (cf. I Cor. II:23; I5:I,3; Gal. I:9,I2; I Thess. 2:I3; 4:I*; 2 Thess. 3:6*)

πεποιθέναι
Phil. I:6 (+ ὅτι), 25*
Phlm. 21*

πειράζειν?
2 Cor. I3:5*

προακούειν
Col. I:5*

προγινώσκειν
Rom. 8:29, II:2* (opp. ἀπωθεῖν)

συνειδέναι
I Cor. 4:4

συνιέναι
Rom. 3:II? (cf. LXX Ps. I3:2 = 52:2, where verb rules τὸν θεόν)

II. Passive Constructions

ἀγνοεῖσθαι
　　I Cor. 14:38* b (variant reading)
　　2 Cor. 6:9*
　　Gal. 1:22

ἀκούεσθαι
　　I Cor. 5:1

ἀνακρίνεσθαι
　　I Cor. 2:14*, 15* b; 4:3*

γινώσκεσθαι
　　I Cor. 3:3*; 14:7*, 9
　　2 Cor. 3:2
　　Gal. 4:9*
　　Phil. 4:5

δοκιμάζεσθαι
　　I Tim. 3:10

ἐπιγινώσκεσθαι
　　I Cor. 13:12* b
　　2 Cor. 6:9*

εὑρίσκεσθαι
　　Rom. 7:10; 10:20 (Isa. 65:1)
　　I Cor. 4:2*; 15:15
　　2 Cor. 5:32; 11:12; 12:20b
　　Gal. 2:17
　　Phil. 2:7?; 3:9*?

καθορᾶσθαι
　　Rom. 1:20?*

μωραίνεσθαι
  Rom. 1:22*

νοεῖσθαι
  Rom. 1:20*

τυφοῦσθαι
  I Tim. 6:4*? (cf. 3:6 and 2 Tim. 3:4)

III. Ruling a Clause
   (relative clauses excluded)

(I) clause introduced by ὅτι

ἀγνοεῖν
  (a) οὐ θέλω (- ομεν ὑμᾶς ἀγνοεῖν, ἀδελφοί, ὅτι (cf. I Cor.
      12:1; I Thess. 4:13)
      Rom. 1:13; 11:25*?
      I Cor. 10:1
      2 Cor. 1:8*
  (b) ἢ ἀγνοεῖτε ὅτι;
      Rom. 6:3; 7:1*
  (c) ἀγνοῶν ὅτι
      Rom. 2:4

ἀκούειν
  Gal. 1:23*?
  Phil. 2:26

βλέπειν
  2 Cor. 7:8

γινώσκειν
  (a) finite verb + ὅτι
      I Cor. 3 :20 ? (Ps. 94:11)
      2 Cor. 8:9?; 13:6*
      Gal. 3:7
      2 Tim. 3:1?
  (b) γινώσκειν ὑμᾶς βούλομαι, ἀδελφοί, ὅτι
      Phil. 1:12

(c) γινώσκοντες ὅτι
   Rom. 6:6?
   Eph. 5:5*

εἰδέναι
   (a) finite verb + ὅτι
      Rom. 2 :2 ; 3 :19 ; 7 :14, 18 ; 8 :22,28* ; 14 :14* ; 15 :29
      1 Cor. 8 :1*, 4* ; 12 :2* ; 16 :15 ?
      2 Cor. 5 :1 ; 11 :11 ?, 31 ; 12 :3-4 ? (οἶδα ... ἄνθρωπον ... ὅτι
         ἡρπάγη)
      Gal. 4:13
      Phil. 1:19,25*; 4:15
      1 Thess. 2:1*?; 3:3*; 5:2
      1 Tim. 1:8*
      2 Tim. 1:15?
   (b) οὐκ οἴδατε ὅτι; (cf. Rom. 11:2)
      Rom. 6:16
      1 Cor. 3:16; 5:6; 6:2, 3, 9, 15, 16, 19; 9:13,24
   (c) θέλω ὑμᾶς εἰδέναι ὅτι
      1 Cor. 11:3 (cf. Col. 2:1)
   (d) εἰδότες ὅτι
      Rom. 5:3; 6:9; 13:11?
      1 Cor. 15:58
      2 Cor. 1:7*; 4:14; 5:6
      Gal. 2:16
      Eph. 6:8,9
      Phil. 1:16
      Col. 3:24; 4:1
      1 Thess. 1:4*? (ὅτι in verse 5)
   (e) εἰδὼς ὅτι (cf. 2 Tim. 1:4, μεμνημένος)
      1 Tim. 1:9*?
      2 Tim. 2:23; 3:14 (ὅτι in verse 15)
      Titus 3:11
      Phlm. 21*

ἐπιγινώσκειν
   Rom. 1:32?
   1 Cor. 14:37*?
   2 Cor. 1:13* b (ὅτι in verse 14), 14?; 13:5*?

ἰδεῖν
>Gal. 2:7 (ἰδόντες ὅτι, cf. verse 9), 14?

κρίνειν?
>2 Cor. 5:14? (κρίναντος τοῦτο,ὅτι)

μνημονεύειν
>2 Thess. 2:5 (οὐ μνημονεύετε ὅτι)

πεπεῖσθαι/πεποιθέναι
>Rom. 8:38; 14:14*; 15:14*
>2 Cor. 2:3?
>Gal. 5:10?
>Phil. 1:6?; 2:24
>2 Thess. 3:4?
>2 Tim. 1:5*, 12*

προιδεῖν
>Gal. 3:8?

>(2) clause introduced by τί (ς)

γνωρίζειν
>Phil. 1:22

δοκιμάζειν
>Rom. 12:2*
>Eph. 5:10

εἰδέναι
>Rom. 8:26?, 27*; 11:2
>1 Cor. 7:16a,b; 14:16
>Eph. 1:18-19*
>1 Thess. 4:2

εὑρίσκειν
>Rom. 4:1?

καταλαμβάνεσθαι
>Eph. 3:18*

συνιέναι
    Eph. 5:17*

(3) miscellaneous

ἀγνοεῖν
    οὐ θέλω ὑμὰς ἀγοεῖν περί
    I Cor. 12:8*
    I Thess. 4:13 (cf. 5:1f.).

ἀκούειν
    I Cor. 11:18
    2 Thess. 3:22? (acc. ptc. = ind. discourse)

βλέπειν
    I Cor. 3:10

γινώσκειν
    I Cor. 13:9*, 12*

εἰδέναι
    I Cor. 1:16
    2 Cor. 13:2b,c,d,3b,c
    Phil. 4:12 1,b
    Col. 2:1 (θέλω ὑμὰς εἰδέναι ἡλίκον
        Cf. I Cor. 11:3); 4:6
    I Thess. 1:5; 4:4
    2 Thess. 3:7
    I Tim. 3:5, 15
    2 Tim. 3:14* (+ ὅτι, verse 15)

μανθάνειν
    Phil. 4:11*
    I Tim. 5:4,13
    Titus 3:14

μυεῖσθαι
    Phil. 4:12*

νοεῖν
 I Tim. 1:7

πειράζειν
 2 Cor. 13:5*?

IV. Absolute Uses

ἀγνοεῖν
 I Tim. 1:13

ἀκούειν
 Rom. 10:14b, 18*; (Isa. 6:10?); 15:21* (Isa. 52:15)
 I Cor. 14:2?
 2 Tim. 4:17?

βλέπειν / ὄψεσθαι
 Rom. 11:8* (Isa. 29:10), 10* (Ps. 69:23); 15:21* (Isa. 52:15)
 I Cor. 13:12*

γινώσκειν
 Rom. 10:19*
 I Cor. 8:2b,c

εἰδέναι
 2 Cor. 11:11?; 12:2d?, 3c?

 καθὼς οἴδατε
  I Thess. 2:2*, 5*, 11 (καθάπερ); 3:4* *cf. 1:5)

ἐπιγινώσκειν
 I Cor. 13:12*a

μανθάνειν
 I Cor. 14:31,35
 I Tim. 2:11

συνιέναι
 Rom. 3:11 (cf. LXX Ps. 13:2 = 52:2, where verb rules); 15:21* (Isa. 52:15)
 2 Cor. 10:12

APPENDIX D

Perhaps the most detailed description of Gnosticism is given by T. P. van Bauren, "Towards a Definition of Gnosticism," in U. Bianci (ed.), *Le Origini dello Gnosticismo* as cited by Edwin Yamauchi in *Pre-Christian Gnosticism* (Grand Rapids: Wm. B. Eerdmans Publishing Company, 1973), pp. 14,15:

1. 'Gnosis considered as knowledge is not primarily intellectual, but is based upon revelation and is necessary for the attainment of full salvation.'

2. 'There is an essential connection between the concept of gnosis as it appears in gnosticism and the concept of time and space that is found there. . . .'

3. 'Gnosticism claims to have a revelation of its own which is essentially secret . . . .'

4. 'The Old Testament is usually rejected with more or less force. If not fully rejected it is interpreted allegorically. The same method of exegesis is as a rule chosen for the New Testament.'

5. 'God is conceived as transcendent . . . . God is conceived as beyond the comprehension of human thought and at the same time as the invariably good . . . . Nearly always evil is inherent in matter in the manner of a physical quality. The cosmological opposition between God and matter is correlated with the ethical opposition of good and evil. God's transcendence may be qualified by the appearance of various beings intermediate between God and the Cosmos, usually called aeons. These beings are as a rule conceived as divine emanations.'

6. 'The world is regarded with a completely pessimistic view. The cosmos was not created by God, but, at most, it is the work of a demiurge who made the world either against God's will, or in ignorance of it . . . .'

7. 'In the world and in mankind pneumatic and material elements are mixed. The pneumatic elements have their origin in God and are the cause of the desire to return to God . . . .'

8. 'Human beings are divided into three classes, according to whether they have gnosis or not. The pneumatics, who possess full gnosis, are by their nature admitted to full salvation. Those who have only pistis ("faith"), may at least attain a certain degree of salvation. Those who are fully taken up with the material world have no chance of salvation at all.'

9. 'Gnosticism makes a clear difference between pistis and gnosis.'

10. 'The essentially dualistic world-view leads as a rule to an extremely ascetic system of ethics, but in some cases we find an "umwertung aller Werte" expressed in complete libertinisim.

11. 'Gnosticism is a religion of revolt.'

12. 'Gnosticism appeals to the desire to belong to an elite.'

13. 'In connection with the basic dualism there is a strong tendency to differentiate between the Heavenly Saviour and the human shape of Jesus of Nazareth. This has led to varying solutions of which docetism is the most prominent one.'

14. 'In most systems Christ is regarded as the great point of reversal in the cosmic process. As evil has come into existence by the fall of a former aeon, so Christ ushers in salvation because he proclaims the unknown God, the good God who had remained a stranger until that moment.'

15. 'In connection with the person of the Saviour we often find the conception of the salvator salvatus or salvandus (the "redeemed re-deemer").'

16. 'In connection with the basic dualism salvation is usually conceived as a complete severing of all ties between the world and the spiritual part of man. This is exemplified in the myth of the ascension of the soul.'

APPENDIX E

The conclusions drawn by Edwin Yamauchi in *Pre-Christian Gnosticism* present a fair and balanced assessment concerning the issue of Gnostic origins and development. His concluding comments as expressed in the above work follow as stated on pages 184-86:

> In conclusion, we have seen how the imposing scholarly edifice of Reitzenstein's and Bultmann's pre-Christian Gnosticism is but little more than an elaborate multi-storied, many-roomed house of cards, whose foundations have been shaken, some of whose structures need buttressing and others have collapsed, leaving a mass of debris with but few solid timbers fit for use in reconstruction.

> At this point, it would seem best to follow Wilson in accepting the presence of an incipient Gnosticism slightly later than the genesis of Christianity. As Wilson points out, 'It therefore seems a legitimate inference that the origins of Gnosticism proper are pre-Johannine, although here we are moving into the shadowy no-man's land between Gnosticism proper and vaguer Gnosis.'

> Schlier has described Gnosticism as the twin brother of Christianity. Such a vivid description, however, gives more credit to the originality of Gnosticism than it deserves. As both Rudolph and Bianchi have noted, Gnosticism always appears as a parasite, 'Nowhere do we find a pure form of Gnosticism, always it is built on earlier, pre-existing religions or on their traditions.'

> Even if we may admit that Paul and John interacted with and combated a rudimentary form of Gnosticism, there is no convincing evidence to uphold the view that Christianity derived as much from Gnosticism as Gnosticism derived from Christianity. As MacRae points out, 'Whatever their debt to nascent Gnosticism, both Paul and John evolved doctrines of Christian Gnosis that could well have been partly inspired by elements current in the syncretistic world about them but are certainly original because they focus on the person of Christ.'

For some scholars, such as Jonas, the priority of Christianity or of Gnosticism may not be a matter of much importance. For the Christian New Testament scholar it is of considerable importance because of the possibility of influence or dependence. No one, of course, can rule out a priori the possibility of the adaptation of a pre-existing pagan or Jewish Gnosticism by the early Christians. It seems fairly clear that some of the Psalms of the Old Testament, for example, made use of demythologized Ugaritic literary motifs without any reflection upon the essence of Jehovah's revelation. There is no inherent reason why the New Testament writers could not have used non-Christian materials also. But in the case of the Old Testament we have Ugaritic texts which are indisputably older. In the case of the New Testament texts we have no Gnostic texts which are older, and the evidences which have been adduced to prove the priority of Gnosticism over Christianity have been weighed in this study and found wanting.

APPENDIX F

The following account is related by W. B. Godbey in *Commentary on the New Testament*, Vol. V (Cincinnati: Revivalist Office, 1899 copyright), pp. 22-24, concerning the salvation of an Indian chief who had not heard the Gospel:

> Captain John Smith, a cultured Episcopalian, during his captivity with the Indians, after the old chief had adopted him as his son and successor, was left in charge of him and his old wife and little grandson, while all the balance went off to war. During a terrible wintry storm, when a great sleet everywhere covered the deep snow, the loud roar of whose breaking beneath the feet entirely disqualified him to get in gunshot of the wild animals on which they were all dependent for their daily food, day after day the young Englishman returns at nightfall from a laborious all-day walk over the ice fields, crushing beneath his feet and letting him down into the deep snow, weary and forlorn, faint with hunger and fatigue. Every evening the venerable chief lying flat on his back on his bear-skin, prostrate with rheumatism, delivers his adopted son a profitable exhortation on the patience and humiliation requisite to qualify a soul at life's end to ascend about the snow clouds, and dwell in the presence of the Great Spirit forever. Finally John concludes that they are all going to starve to death in a pile. Consequently, with much regret in his own heart to leave those people to die alone, he set out apparently as usual on a hunting excursion, but with his mind made up to escape and make his way back to Jamestown. While thus trudging along, seeing a herd of buffaloes at a great distance, taking position in concealment, he prays God to send them within gun-shot, as he had had nothing to eat for a week but some broth made from the bones of a wild-cat, which the vultures had picked, and they had recovered from beneath the snow. Sure enough, his prayer is answered and the herd comes roaring along near by. He fires away and downs a fat heifer. Running, he cuts some meat and satisfies his awful hunger by eating it blood-raw. Then supplying himself with some of the food to eat on his journey, his heart turns back with incorrigible sympathy for those poor people he had left to die. Consequently, loading himself with the meat, he wends his way back to the wigwam, arriving at nightfall, and saluted by the venerable chief, lying on his back, "O, my son, I knew you would bring it to-day. Oeneah (the name of his God) told me so." Smith wanted to hand him some of it raw to eat at once. "O, no, my son, I am not in a hurry." "Well," says Smith, "I will broil you some on the coals." "O, no, I prefer it stewed. While it is cooking I want you to sit down that I may talk to you about

the great spirit, Oeneah, who always takes good care of his children." Smith felt himself a missionary among them, and had been teaching them the Christian religion the best he could from the Bible. Now he finds, to his surprise, that the old Indian, who had spent his life in savagedom, knew much more about the Lord, and his salvation, than he did. I mention this to demonstrate a case of a heathen who was intelligently saved, walking with God and bearing the fruits of the Spirit.

ENDNOTES

PART I

[1] Tom Allen, *A Closer Look at Dr. Laura* (Camp Hill, PA: Horizon Books, 1998), 181.

[2] Ibid., 183.

[3] Ibid., 184, 5.

[4] Much of the historical sketch for this period is drawn from Peter D. Arnott, *An Introduction to the Greek World* (London: Macmillan and Company Limited, 1967), 18-38.

[5] M. I. Finley, *The Ancient Greeks* (New York: The Viking Press, 1965), 1.

[6] Finley Hooper, *Greek Realities* (London: Rupert Hart-Davis Limited, 1968), 39.

[7] Arnott, 21.

[8] Finley, 1.

[9] Hooper, 43.

[10] Finley, 2.

[11] Hooper, 64,65.

[12] Finley, 16.

[13] Ibid., 69.

[14] The following survey is especially indebted to Finley, 14-30.

[15] Ibid., 20.

[16] Arnott, 30.

[17] Ibid., 34.

[18] Hans Jonas, *The Gnostic Religion* (Boston: Beacon Press, 1958), 18,19.

[19] Edith Hamilton, *The Greek Way* (New York: W. W. Norton & Company, Inc., 1964 reprint), 22.

[20] Hooper, p. 7.

[21] C. M. Bowra, *The Greek Experience* (Cleveland: The World Publishing Company, 1957), p. 4.

[22] Ibid., p. 5.

[23] Ibid., p. 4,5.

[24] Hamilton, p. 22.

[25] F. S. C. Northrop, *The Meeting of East and West* (New York: The Macmillan Company, 1946), pp. 315,316.

[26] The following discussion of both Egypt and India is largely drawn from Edith Hamilton in *The Greek Way*, pp. 17-21.

[27] Ibid., p. 19.

[28] Hamilton, p. 20.

[29] Northrop, p. 294.

[30] Bowra, pp. 20,21.

[31] Ibid, p. 21.

[32] Werner, Jaeger, *Paideia: the Ideals of Greek Culture,* trans. Gilbert Highet (New York: Oxford University Press, 1945), I, p. xiv.

[33] R. F. Earp, *The Way of the Greeks* (London: Oxford University Press, 1929), p. 43.

[34] Ibid., pp. 43-46.

[35] Hooper, p. 2.

[36] Ibid.

[37] Edwyn Bevan, *Hellenism and Christianity* (Freeport: Books for Libraries Press, Inc., 1967 reprint), p. 36.

[38] Ibid., p. 14

[39] Ibid., pp. 16,17.

[40] Bowra, p. 165.

[41] Hamilton, p. 34.

[42] *Timaeus,*, VII.22.C (The Loeb Classical Library).

[43] Hamilton, p. 23.

[44] Hooper, p. 106.

[45] *Laws* II 656-7 (Loeb Classical Library).

[46] Hamilton, pp. 39,40.

[47] Hooper, p. 107.

[48] Hamilton, p. 41.

[49] Bowra, pp. 124,125.

[50] Hamilton, p. 27.

[51] *The Republic* IV. 435 E (Loeb Classical Library).

[52] The discussion under this heading is indebted to Brown's chapter on "The Place of Reason," pp. 165-185, in *The Greek Experience.*

[53] Cited by Hamilton, p. 20.

[54] Ibid.

[55] Bowra, p. 166.

[56] Ibid., pp. 176,177.

[57] Hooper, p. 263.

[58] Ibid.

[59] Hamilton, p. 28.

[60] Glover, T. R., *The World of the New Testament* (New York: The Macmillan Co., 1931), p. 53.

[61] Hooper, pp. 263,265.

[62] Jaeger, III, p. 5.

[63] Bowra, p. 178.

[64] Ibid., p. 179.

[65] Hamilton, p. 28.

[66] *The Republic* 509 D.

[67] Bowra, p. 166.

[68] Jaeger, I, p. xxi.

[69] Jaeger, I, p. xxi.

[70] Ibid., p. xxii.

[71] Bowra, p. 175.

[72] Finley, p. 109.

[73] See also Jaeger for a clear explanation of Socrates' dialogue on the Idea of Good and related matters, from which part of the following discussion is drawn.

[74] *The Republic* 505A.

[75] Ibid., 379 A,B.

[76] Ibid., 379 C.

[77] Ibid., 508 B.

[78] Ibid., 508 D.

[79] Jaeger, II, p. 284.

[80] *The Republic*, 511 B.C.

[81] Ibid, 511 C, D.

[82] Ibid., 511 D, E.

[83] Ibid., 515 B.C.

[84] *The Republic*, 517 B.C.

[85] *Epistles*, VII 341-345.

[86] Jaeger, II, p. 230.

[87] William Barclay, *The Letters of John and Jude* (Philadelphia: The Westminster Press, 1960), p. 48.

[88] Jaeger, II, p. 285.

[89] Ibid.

[90] *The Republic*, II, xxvi.

[91] Jaeger, II, p. 285.

[92] *The Republic* 379 C

[93] Jaeger, II, p. 173.

[94] *Timaeus* 28C.

[95] *Laws* 966 C-969 B.

[96] The following discussion on the origin of Greek religion is especially drawn from Arnott, *An Introduction to the Greek World*, pp. 42-45.

[97] Hamilton, p. 41.

[98] Bowra, p. 45.

[99] J. Gresham Machen, *The Origin of Paul's Religion* (Grand Rapids: Wm. B. Eerdmans Publishing Company, 1978 reprint), p. 214.

[100] Hamilton, p. 173.

[101] Bowra, p. 52.

[102] Hamilton, p. 174.

[103] Finley, p. 31.

[104] Bowra, p. 59.

[105] The survey of the twelve Olympian deities is particularly drawn from Arnott, *An Introduction to the Greek World*, pp. 45-50.

[106] Finley, p. 33.

[107] Bowra, pp. 57,58.

[108] Ibid., p. 57.

[109] Cited by Hamilton, p. 178.

[110] Ibid.

[111] *The Republic* 379

[112] Machen, p. 219.

[113] S. Angus, *The Mystery-Religions and Christianity* (New York: Charles Scribner's Sons, 1925), p. 11.

[114] Ibid.

[115] Bowra, p. 44.

[116] Cited by Arnott, p. 65.

[117] Finley, p. 114.

[118] Glover, p. 43.

[119] Machen, pp. 219,200.

[120] Arnott, pp. 67,68.

[121] Hamilton, p. 178.

[122] Angus, p. 13.

[123] Arnott, pp. 55,56.

[124] Ibid., pp. 56,57.

[125] Machen, pp. 215,216.

[126] Ibid., p. 215.

[127] Arnott, p. 55.

[128] C. H. Dodd, *The Interpretation of the Fourth Gospel* (London: The Cambridge University Press, 1958), p. 154.

[129] Angus, p. 43.

[130] Machen, p. 235.

[131] Barclay, p. 49.

[132] Ibid.

[133] Machen., p. 218.

[134] Joscelyn Godwin, *Mystery Religions in the Ancient World* (San Francisco: Harper & Row, Publishers, 1981), p. 33.

[135] Arnott, p. 70.

[136] Barclay, pp. 49,50.

[137] Machen, p. 233.

[138] Gilbert Murray, *Five Stages of Greek Religion* (New York: AMS Press, 1978 reprint), p. 155.

[139] Angus, p. 52.

[140] Ibid., p. 55.

[141] Ibid., pp. 63,64.

[142] Godwin, p. 35.

[143] Ibid., p. 34.

[144] The above survey was largely drawn from *The Homeric Hymn to Demeter*, trans. Thelma Sargent (New York: W. W. Norton & Company, Inc., 1973), pp. 2-14. See also Arnott, pp. 68,69.

[145] Hamilton, p. 179.

[146] Arnott, p. 69.

[147] *De Legibus* XIV 36. (Loeb Classical Library)

[148] *The Frogs*, pp. 153ff.

[149] William Barclay, *The Letters of James and Peter* (Philadelphia: The Westminster Press, 1960), p. 349.

[150] Alan Richardson, *An Introduction to the Theology of the New Testament* (New York: Harper & Row, Publishers, 1958), p. 40.

[151] W. T. Purkiser, R. S. Taylor, and W. H. Taylor, *God, Man and Salvation* (Kansas City: Beacon Hill Press, 1977), p. 44.

[152] Ibid., p. 45.

[153] Purkiser, p. 44.

[154] *The Interpreter's Dictionary of the Bible* (New York: Abingdon, 1962), p. 44.

PART II

[1] Richard J. Erickson, "Oida and Ginosko and Verbal Aspect in Pauline Usage," *Westminster Theological Journal*, XLIV (1982), 112.

[2] E. D.Schmitz, "Knowledge, Experience, Ignorance," *The New International Dictionary of New Testament Theology*, ed. Colin Brown (Grand Rapids: Zondervan Publishing House, 1975), II, 392.

[3] Henry George Liddell and Robert Scott, "γιγνώσκω," *A Greek-English Lexicon* (Oxford: University Press, 1953), p. 350.

[4] Homer, *The Iliad* XII.272. (The Loeb Classical Library).

[5] Homer, *The Iliad* V. 128, trans. A. T. Murray.

[6] Ibid., trans. Robert Fitzgerald.

[7] Herodotus, VI.85.

[8] R. Bultmann, "γινώσκω," *Theological Dictionary of the New Testament* (1981), I, p. 690.

[9] Homer, *The Odyssey* XV.532.

[10] Schmitz, p. 392.

[11] Homer, *The Odyssey*, XV.536,537.

[12] J. H. Thayer, *A Greek-English Lexicon of the New Testament* (Grand Rapids: Baker Book House, 1980), p. 118.

[13] See C. H. Dodd, *The Interpretation of the Fourth Gospel* (London: Cambridge University Press, 1958), pp. 151ff.

[14] Bultmann, p. 691.

[15] Ibid.

[16] Schmitz, p. 392.

[17] Thucydides, *History of the Peloponnesian War* I.25.1. (The Loeb Classical Library).

[18] Bultmann, p. 691.

[19] Ibid., p. 692.

[20] See A. H. Newman, *A Manual of Church History* (Valley Forge: Judson Press, 1964), I pp. 23,24.

[21] James Hope Moulton and George Milligan, *The Vocabulary of the Greek Testament* (Grand Rapids: Wm. B. Eerdmans Publishing Co., 1963), p. 127.

[22] Schmitz, p. 393.

[23] Edwin Hatch and Henry A. Redpath, *A Concordance to the Septuagint* (Graz-Austria: Akademische Druck-U. Verlagsanstaldt, 1954), I, pp. 267-270.

[24] Schmitz, p. 395.

[25] Ibid.

[26] See James Strong, *The Exhaustive Concordance of the Bible* (New York: Abingdon Press, 1961), pp. 31,45 of Hebrew and Chaldee Dictionary in connection with the coded numerals under "Know" and "Knowledge," especially prepared for those who do not know Hebrew.

[27] Bultmann, p. 697.

[28] O. A. Piper, "Knowledge," *The Interpreter's Dictionary of the Bible* (New York: Abingdon Press, 1962), III, p. 43.

[29] Schmitz, p. 395.

[30] Dodd, p. 160.

[31] Ibid., p. 163.

[32] Ibid.

[33] Schmitz, p. 395.

[34] W. F. Moulton and A.S. Geden, *A Concordance to the Greek Testament* (Edinburgh: T. & T. Clark, 1950), pp. 170-172.

[35] W. F. Arndt and F. W. Gingrich, *A Greek-English Lexicon of the New Testament and other Early Christian Literature* (Chicago: The University of Chicago Press, 1957), pp. 159-161.

[36] Moises Silva, "The Pauline Style As Lexical Choice: ΓΙΝΏΣΚΕΙΝ and Related Verbs," *Pauline Studies*, ed. D. A. Hagner and M. J. Harris (Exeter: The Paternoster Press, LTD, 1980), pp. 197,198.

[37] Moulton and Geden, p. 172.

[38] Mark 5:29 (Eight Translation New Testament).

[39] Mark 5:29 (New American Standard Bible).

[40] Mark 5:29 (New King James Version).

[41] Arndt and Gingrich , pp. 159-161.

[42] Erickson, p. 121.

[43] J. Gresham Machen, *New Testament Greek for Beginners* (New York: The Macmillan Company, 1965), p. 218.

[44] Arndt and Gingrich, p. 558.

[45] Liddell and Scott, p. 483.

[46] Ibid.

[47] Homer, *The Odyssey*, I.337.

[48] Aristophanes, *The Wasps* 376.

[49] Herodotus IV.76.

[50] Wilhelm Michaelis, "ὁράω, εἶδον" *Theological Dictionary of the New Testament* (1981), V, p. 316.

[51] Ibid.

[52] Homer, *The Odyssey* IV.538-540.

[53] Michaelis, p. 317.

[54] Donald W. Burdick, "Οἶδα and Γινώσκω in the Pauline Epistles" *New Dimensions in New Testament Study*, ed. R. N. Longenecker and M. C. Tenney (Grand Rapids: Zondervan Publishing House, 1974), p.344.

[55] Erickson, p. 112.

[56] Michaelis, p. 319.

[57] Moulton and Milligan, p. 439.

[58] Ibid., p. 440.

[59] Ibid., p. 439.

[60] Hatch and Redpath, I, pp. 374,375.

[61] Ibid., pp. 267-270.

[62] Ibid., pp. 374,375.

[63] Ibid., p. 268.

[64] Ibid., p. 375.

[65] Genesis 2:9 (The Septuagint Version).

[66] I kings 20:3 (The Septuagint Version).

[67] Moulton and Geden, pp. 267-270; 170-172.

[68] Ibid., pp. 267-270.

[69] All these figures are derived from an examination of Moulton and Geden, 267.

[70] Moulton and Geden, 267-270.

[71] William Henry Simcox, *The Writers of the New Testament* (Winona Lake: Alpha Publications, 1980), 71.

[72] Moulton and Geden, 268,269.

[73] Ibid., 269.

[74] Thayer, 117-118; 174.

[75] Arndt and Gingrich, 558.

[76] W. E. Vine, *An Expository Dictionary of New Testament Words* (Westwood: Fleming H. Revell Company, 1961), 298.

[77] Liddell and Scott, 627.

[78] Xenophon, *Cyropaedia* VIII.1.33.

[79] Homer, *The Odyssey* XXIV.216,217.

[80] Thucydides, *History of the Peloponnesian War* I.132. (Loeb Classical Library).

[81] Thucydides, III.57.

[82] J. Armitage Robinson, *St. Paul's Epistle to the Ephesians* (London: Macmillan and Co., Limited, 1909), 248.

[83] Moulton and Milligan, 236.

[84] Polybius, *Histories* III.32.8.

[85] Hatch and Redpath, 517,518.

[86] Ibid., 518.

[87] Ibid.

[88] Moulton and Geden, 365,366.

[89] Ibid., 170-72.

[90] G. Abbott-Smith, *A Manual Greek Lexicon of the New Testament* (New York: Charles Scribner's Sons, 1936), p. 168.

[91] Thayer, 237.

[92] Vine, 299.

[93] Arndt and Gingrich, 290-91.

[94] Thayer, 236.

[95] Liddell and Scott, 658,659.

[96] Herodotus III.134.

[97] Homer, *The Iliad*, XXIII.705.

[98] Moulton and Milligan, 245.

[99] Hatch and Redpath, 529.

[100] Moulton and Geden, 371.

[101] Arndt and Gingrich, 300.

[102] Thayer, 118.

[103] Donald A. Nash, *New Testament Word Studies* (Grayson: Witness Press, 1982), 201.

196   *Is God Knowable?*

[104] Liddell and Scott, 1718.

[105] Homer, *The Odyssey* IV.76.

[106] Herodotus, 1.24.

[107] Aristophanes, *The Plutus* 45.

[108] Hans Conzelmann, "συνίημι," *Theological Dictionary of the New Testament* (1982), VII, 888.

[109] Ibid.

[110] Moulton and Milligan, 607-8.

[111] Hatch and Redpath, 1316-17.

[112] Conzelmann, 890.

[113] Moulton and Geden, 922,923.

[114] Thayer, 605.

[115] Thayer, 118.

[116] Nash, 202.

[117] Thayer, 118.

[118] Liddell and Scott, 1718.

[119] See Homer, *The Iliad* 1.8; VII.210.

[120] Littell and Scott, 1718.

[121] Ibid.

[122] Liddell and Scott, 365.

[123] Ibid.

[124] Moulton and Milligan, 129,130.

[125] Ibid., 129.

[126] Hatch and Redpath, p. 273.

[127] Moulton and Geden, 173,174.

[128] Liddell and Scott, 627.

[129] Robinson, 248.

[130] Moulton and Milligan, 237.

[131] Ibid.

[132] Hatch and Redpath, 518.

[133] Moulton and Geden, 366.

[134] Burdick, 344.

[135] Erickson, 112.

[136] Thucydides, 1.69.3.

[137] J. B. Lightfoot, *Notes on the Epistles of St. Paul* (Winona Lake: Alpha Publications, 1979), 179.

[138] Ibid.

[139] J. B. Lightfoot, *St. Paul's Epistle to the Galatians* (London: Macmillan and Co., Limited, 1921), 171.

[140] Cited by Burdick, 345.

[141] B. F. Westcott, *The Epistles of St. John* (Grand Rapids: Wm. B. Eerdmans Publishing Co., 1982 reprint), 46.

[142] Ibid.

[143] Cited by Burdick, 346.

[144] Erickson, III.

[145] Burdick, 345.

[146] Cited by Burdick, 345.

[147] Moulton and Milligan, 439.

[148] Dodd, 152.

[149] Heinrich Seesemann, "οἶδα," *Theological Dictionary of the New Testament* (1981), V, 116.

[150] Leon Morris, *The Gospel According to John* (Grand Rapids: Wm. B. Eerdmans Publishing Co., 1971), 206.

[151] Cited by Morris, 206.

[152] Westcott, *The Gospel According to St. John*, 202.

[153] Burdick, 346.

[154] Nigel Turner, *Grammatical Insights Into the New Testament* (Edinburgh: T. T. Clark, 1977), 152,153.

[155] Seesemann, 117.

[156] Nash, 200.

[157] Ibid.

[158] Ibid.

[159] Burdick, 334-56.

[160] Ibid, 346.

[161] Burdick, 346-7.

[162] Erickson, III.

[163] Ibid., 112.

[164] Burdick, 353

[165] Ibid., 354.

[166] See Appendix B for specific distribution of verses in each classification.

[167] Burdick, 354.

[168] Silva, 184-207.

[169] Ibid., 185.

[170] Ibid.

[171] Ibid., 186,187.

[172] See Appendix C for Silva's treatment of grammatical structures along with verse listings under each.

[173] Silva, 201.

[174] Ibid., 186.

[175] Silva, 186.

[176] Ibid., 201, 202.

[177] Burdick, 347.

[178] Silva, 201.

[179] Ibid., 202.

[180] Burdick, 350.

[181] Silva, 202.

[182] Burdick, 350.

[183] Ibid.

[184] Burdick, 352.

[185] Silva, 202.

[186] Ibid., 200.

[187] Erickson, 110-22.

[188] Ibid., 113.

[189] Ibid., 114.

[190] Ibid., 118.

[191] Ibid., 116,120.

[192] Erickson, 120.

[193] Ibid., 121,122.

[194] J. B. Lightfoot, *Saint Paul's Epistle to the Philippians* (Grand Rapids: Zondervan Publishing House, 1965), 86.

[195] Cited by Robert E. Picirelli, "The Meaning of Epignosis," *The Evangelical Quarterly* XLVII (1975), 87,88.

[196] William Barclay, *The Letters of James and Peter* (Philadelphia: The Westminster Press, 1960), 347,348.

[197] Ibid.

[198] Robinson, 249.

[199] Ibid., 254.

[200] H. A. W. Meyer, *Critical and Exegetical Handbook to the Epistles to the Philippians and Colossians* (Peabody: Hendrickson Publishers, Inc., 1983 reprint), 214,215.

[201] Picirelli, 89,90.

[202] Ibid., 91.

[203] Ibid.

[204] Ibid., 92.

[205] Ibid., 90.

[206] Leon Morris, *The First Epistle of Paul to the Corinthians*)Grand Rapids: Wm. B. Eerdmans Publishing Company, 1980), 188.

[207] B. C. Caffin, *The Second Epistle General of Peter*, ed. H. D. M. Spence and Joseph S. Exell, The Pulpit Commentary, Vol. XXII (Grand Rapids: Wm. B. Eerdmans Publishing Company, 1962 reprint), 2.

[208] R. J. Knowling, *The Acts of the Apostles*, ed. W. Robertson Nicol, The Expositor's Greek Testament, Vol. II (Grand Rapids: Wm. B. Eerdmans Publishing Company, 1980 reprint), 407.

[209] Ibid.

[210] Nash, 201.

[211] Ibid.

[212] Ibid.

PART III

[1] See *The Nag Hammadi Library*, edited by James M. Robinson (San Francisco: Harper & Row, Publishers, 1977).

[2] A. D. Nock, "Gnosticism," *Harvard Theological Review*, 57 (October, 1964), 274.

[3] See Edwin Yamauchi, *Pre-Christian Gnosticism* (Grand Rapids: Wm. B. Eerdmans Publishing Company, 1973), v.

[4] R. M. Grant, *Gnosticism and Early Christianity* (New York: Columbia University Press, 1959), 7.

[5] Jacques Lacarriere, *The Gnostics* (New York: E. P. Dutton, 1977), 9.

[6] Yamauchi, 13,14.

[7] Ibid., vi.

[8] Ibid.

[9] Robert M. Grant, *Gnosticism* (New York : AMS Press, 1978 reprint), 16.

[10] S. Angus, *The Mystery-Religions* (New York: Dover Publications, Inc., 1975 reprint), 52.

[11] Richard Reitzenstein, *Hellenistic Mystery-Religions*, trans. John E. Steely (Pittsburgh: The Pickwick Press, 1978), 83.

[12] R. Martin Pope, "Faith and Knowledge in Pauline and Johannine Thought," *The Expository Times*, XLI (1930), 421.

[13] Nock, 256.

[14] R. McL. Wilson, *The Gnostic Problem* (London: A. R. Mowbray & Co. Limited, 1958), 69.

[15] Lacarriere, 10.

[16] See Appendix D; also see Geddes MacGregor, *Gnosis* (Wheaton: The Theosophical Publishing House, 1979), 37-52 for a critique of van Baaren's sixteen characteristics of Gnosticism.

[17] Werner, Foerster, *Gnosis*, English translation edited by R. McL. Wilson (London: Oxford University Press, 1972), 2,3.

[18] Ibid., 2.

[19] E. D. Schmitz, "Knowledge, Experience, Ignorance," *The New International Dictionary of New Testament Theology*, ed. Colin Brown (Grand Rapids: Zondervan Publishing House, 1975), II, 394.

[20] Cited by Yamauchi, 20.

[21] Ibid., 59,60.

[22] Jean Danielou, *The Theology of Jewish Christianity*, trans. And ed. John A. Baker (Chicago: The Henry Regnery Company, 1964), 73.

[23] Yamauchi, 60.

[24] Wilson, 100,101.

[25] Virginia Corwin, *St. Ignatius and Christianity in Antioch* (New Haven: Yale University Press, 1960), viii.

[26] Yamauchi, 69.

[27] C. H. Dodd, *The Bible and the Greeks* (London: Hodder and Stoughton, 1954), 209.

[28] Yamauchi, 69.

[29] Ibid., 70.

[30] Ibid., 71,72.

[31] C. H. Dodd, *The Interpretation of the Fourth Gospel* (London: Cambridge University Press, 1958), 115,116.

[32] Cited by Yamauchi, 118.

[33] Stephen Neill, *The Interpretation of the New Testament* (London: Oxford University Press, 1964), 178.

[34] Dodd, *The Interpretation of the Fourth Gospel*, 130.

[35] Yamauchi, 144.

[36] W. D. Davies, "Knowledge in the Dead Sea Scrolls and Matthew 11:25-30," *Harvard Theological Review*, XLVI (July, 1953), 119-28.

[37] The above passages in the DSS have been taken from various translations. See A. Dupont-Sommer, *The Essene Writings from Qumran*, trans. T. H. Gaster (New York: Doubleday & Company, 1964.) Also see "The Dead Sea Manual of Discipline," *Bulletin of the American Schools of Oriental Research*, trans. W. H. Brownlee (Jerusalem: American Schools of Oriental Research, 1951).

[38] See E. D. Schmitz, 397.

[39] See Yamauchi, 155.

[40] Ibid., 153,154.

[41] Cited by Yamauchi, 161.

[42] Danielou, 54.

[43] Ibid., 70.

[44] Yamauchi, 161,162.

[45] See Yamauchi, 30.

[46] Rudolf Bultmann, *The Gospel of John, a Commentary*, trans. G. R. Beasley-Murray, R. W. N. Hoare and J. K. Riches (Philadelphia: The Westminster Press, 1971), 8.

[47] See Yamauchi, 30.

[48] W. F. Albright, *New Horizons in Biblical Research* (London: Oxford University Press, 1966), 46.

[49] See Davies, 113-139.

[50] Cited by Yamauchi, 36.

[51] Wilhelm Bousset, *Kyrios Christians*, trans. John E. Steely (Nashville: Abingdon Press, 1970), 254.

[52] See Yamauchi, 37.

[53] Ibid., 39.

[54] Walter Schmithals, *Gnosticism in Corinth*, trans. John E. Steely (Nashville: Abingdon Press, 1971), 247.

[55] Cited by Yamauchi, 41.

[56] Nock, 277.

[57] J. B. Lightfoot, *St. Paul's Epistles to the Colossians and to Philemon* (Grand Rapids: Zondervan Publishing Company, 1965), 113.

[58] See Yamauchi, 46.

[59] Ibid., 45.

[60] G. Quispel, "Gnosticism and the New Testament," *The Bible in Modern Scholarship*, ed. J. Philip Hyatt (Nashville: Abingdon Press, 1965), 255.

[61] Cited by Yamauchi, 50.

[62] Ibid., 51.

[63] See Yamauchi, 51,52.

[64] Donald Guthrie, *New Testament Introduction-Hebrews to Revelation* (Chicago: Inter-Varsity Press, 1966), 89.

[65] Rudolf Bultmann, *Theology of the New Testament*, I, trans. Kendrick Grobel (New York: Charles Scribner's Sons, 1951), 174.

[66] See Yamauchi, 52,53.

[67] Ibid., 53.

[68] Ibid.

[69] Guthrie, 205.

[70] Yamauchi, 170.

[71] Neill, 177.

[72] Yamauchi, 171.

[73] Neill, 177.

[74] Yamauchi, 174.

[75] Ibid., 173.

[76] Ibid., 179-81.

[77] Ibid., 182.

[78] Ibid., 184

[79] W. B. Godbey, *Commentary on the New Testament*, V (Cincinnati: Revivalist Office, 1899), 21.

[80] H. Orton Wiley, *Christian Theology*, Vol. I (Kansas City: Beacon Hill Press, 1960), 126.

[81] Ibid.

[82] See C. E. B. Cranfield, *The Epistle to the Romans*, Vol. I, eds. J. A. Emerton and C. E. B. Cranfield, *The International Critical Commentary* (Edinburgh: T. & T. Clark Limited, 1975), 113.

[83] A. W. Meyer, *The Epistle to the Romans*, Vol. V, trans. J. C. Moore, E. Johnson, and W. P. Dickson (Peabody: Hendrickson Publishers, Inc., 1983 reprint), 57.

[84] Cranfield, 113.

[85] James Denney, *St. Paul's Epistle to the Romans,* ed. W. Robertson Nicoll, *The Expositor's Greek Testament,* Vol. II (Grand Rapids: Wm. B. Eerdmans Publishing Company, 1980 reprint), 592.

[86] Willard H. Taylor, "The Knowledge of God," *God, Man and Salvation* (Kansas City: Beacon Hill Press, 1977), 218.

[87] Denney, 592.

[88] This is the position taken by Burton in *Moods and Tenses* as cited by W. Sanday and A. C. Headlam, *The Epistle to the Romans,* eds. C. A. Briggs, S. R. Driver, and A. Plummer, *The International Critical Commentary* (New York: Charles Scribner's Sons, 1904), 44.

[89] James M. Stifler, *The Epistle to the Romans* (Chicago: Moody Press, 1960)., 31.

[90] See C. K. Barrett, *A Commentary on the Epistle to the Romans* (New York: Harper & Row, 1957), 49.

[91] J. A. Beet, *A Commentary on St. Paul's Epistle to the Romans* (Salem: Allegheny Publications, 1982 reprint), 77.

[92] D. D. Whedon, *Commentary on the New Testament,* Vol. III (Salem: Schmul Publishers, 1977 reprint), 306.

[93] John Wesley, *The Works of John Wesley,* Vol. VI (Grand Rapids: Baker Book House, 1978 reprint), 512.

[94] Stifler, 42.

[95] Whedon, 306.

[96] Barrett, 52,53.

[97] Cranfield, 158.

[98] Lewis Johnson, "Paul and the Knowledge of God," *Bibliotheca sacra,* 129 (January-March 1972), 73-74.

[99] Godbey, 21.

[100] Ibid.

[101] Marcus Dods, *The Gospel of St. John,* ed. W. Robertson Nicoll, *The Expositor's Greek Testament,* Vol. I (Grand Rapids: Wm. B. Eerdmans Publishing Company, 1980 reprint), 686.

[102] John Wesley, *Explanatory Notes Upon the New Testament* (Salem, OH: Schmul Publishers, 1976), 213.

[103] John Calvin, *Gospel According to John,* trans. Wm. Pringle, *Calvin's Commentaries* (Grand Rapids: Baker Book House, 1979 reprint), 38.

[104] Ibid.

[105] Cited by Dodd, 686.

[106] Ibid.

[107] B. F. Westcott, *The Gospel According to St. John* (Grand Rapids: Baker Book House, 1980 reprint), 13,14.

[108] Cited by R. J. Knowling, "The Acts of the Apostles," ed. W. Robertson Nicholl, *The Expositors Greek Testament*, Vol. II (Grand Rapids: Wm. B. Eerdmans Publishing Company, 1980 reprint), 259.

[109] Meyer, Vol. IV, 210.

[110] Wesley, *Notes*, 304.

[111] Ibid.

[112] G. Campbell Morgan, *The Acts of the Apostles* (Tappan: Fleming H. Revell Company, copyright, 1924), 281.

[113] Whedon, 136.

[114] Adam Clarke, *Clarke's Commentary*, Vol. I (Nashville: Abingdon Press, n.d.), 764.

[115] Wiley, 135.

[116] Ibid., 140.

[117] Josh McDowell, *Evidence That Demands a Verdict* (San Bernardino: Campus Crusade for Christ, 1972), 115.

[118] Ibid.

[119] Cited by Taylor, 212.

[120] Alan Richardson, *An Introduction to the Theology of the New Testament* (New York: Harper & Row, Publishers, 1958), 43.

[121] Whedon, I, 146.

[122] Westcott, 27.

[123] Ibid.

[124] Whedon, II, 233.

[125] Ibid., IV, 25.

[126] R. E. Howard, "The Epistle to the Galatians," *Beacon Bible Commentary*, Vol. IX (Kansas City: Beacon Hill Press, 1965), 71.

[127] Martin Luther, *A Commentary on St. Paul's Epistle to the Galatians*, trans. Theodore Graebner (Grand Rapids: Zondervan, n.d.), 157.

[128] Denney, 648.

[129] Ibid.

[130] Beet, 226.

[131] Bernard Ramm, *The Witness of the Spirit* (Grand Rapids: Wm. B. Eerdmans Publishing Company, 1960), 52. Unfortunately in his detailed discussion Ramm

entirely omits the viewpoints of Wesley and other Arminian scholars.

[132] Ibid.

[133] Wesley's *Works*, V, 115.

BIBLIOGRAPHY

A. PRIMARY SOURCES

1. Biblical Texts

The Greek New Testament, eds. Barbara Aland, Kurt Aland, Johannes Karavidopoulos, Carlo M. Martini, and Bruce M. Metzger. Fourth Revised Edition. New York: United Bible Societies, 1994.

The Greek New Testament According to the Majority Text, eds. Zane C. Hodges and Arthur L. Farstad. 2nd ed. New York: Thomas Nelson Publishers, 1985.

2. Jewish Literature

The Dead Sea Scriptures, trans. T. H. Gaster. New York: Doubleday, 1964.

Dupont-Sommer, A. The Essene Writings from Qumran, trans. G. Vermes. Gloucester: Peter Smith, 1973.

The Nag Hammadi Library, ed. James M. Robinson. San Francisco : Harper & Row, 1977.

3. Secular Literature

Aristophanes. The Frogs, ed. G. P. Goold; trans. Benjamin Bickley Rogers. Cambridge: Harvard University Press, 1979.

Cicero. De Legibus, ed. G. P. Goold; trans. Clinton Wallen Keyes. Cambridge: Harvard University Press, 1977.

Herodotus, trans. A. D. Godley. New York: G. P. Putnam's Sons, 1922.

Homer. The Iliad, ed. G. P. Goold; trans. A. T. Murray. Cambridge: Harvard University Press, 1978.

Homer. The Odyssey, ed. G. P. Goold; trans. A. T. Murray. Cambridge: Harvard University Press, 1980.

_____. *The Homeric Hymn to Demeter*, trans. Thelma Sargent, New York: W. W. Norton & Company, Inc., 1973.

Plato. *Laws*, ed. E. Capps et al. ; trans. R. G. Bury. London: Wm. Heineman LTD, 1926.

Plato. *The Republic*, ed. T. E. Page et al. ; trans. Paul Shorey. Cambridge: Harvard University Press, 1980.

Plato. *Timaeus*. Ed. T. E. Page et al.; trans. R. G. Bury. London: Wm. Heineman LTD, 1929.

Thucydides. *The History of the Peloponnesian War*, ed. G. P. Goold; trans. Charles Forster Smith. Cambridge: Harvard University Press.

Xenophon. *Cyropaedia*, ed. E. H. Warmington; trans. Walter Miller. Cambridge: Harvard University Press, 1968, I.

B. SECONDARY SOURCES

I. Articles in Reference Works

Bultmann, R. "γινώσκω." *Theological Dictionary of the New Testament*, ed. G. Kittel; trans. and ed. Geoffrey W. Bromley. Grand Rapids: Eerdmans, 1969, I, 689-719.

Caffin, B. C. "The Second Epistle General of Peter." *The Pulpit Commentary*, ed. H. D. M. Spence and Joseph S. Exell. Reprint. Grand Rapids: Eerdmans, 1962, XXII, 2.

Calvin, John. "Gospel According to John." *Calvin's Commentaries*, trans. Wm. Pringle. Reprint. Grand Rapids: Baker, 1979, 38.

Conzelmann, Hans. "συνίημι." *Theological Dictionary of the New Testament*, ed. Gerhard Friedrich; trans. And ed. Geoffrey W. Bromley. Grand Rapids: Eerdmans, 1982, VII, 888.

Cranfield, C. E. B. "The Epistle to the Romans." *The International Critical Commentary*, ed. J. A. Emerton and C. E. B. Cranfield. Edinburgh: T. & T. Clark LTD, 1975, I, 113.

Denney, James. "St. Paul's Epistles to the Romans." *The Expositors Greek Testament*, ed. W. Robertson Nicoll. Reprint. Grand Rapids: Eerdmans, 1980, II, 592-648.

Dods, Marcus. "The Gospel of St. John." *The Expositors Greek Testament*, ed. W. Robertson Nicoll. Reprint. Grand Rapids: Erdmans, 1980, I, 686.

Howard, R. D. "The Epistle to the Galatians." *Beacon Bible Commentary*. Kansas City: Beacon Hill, 1965, IX, 71.

Knowling, R. J. "The Acts of the Apostles," *The Expositor's Greek Testament*, ed. W. Robertson Nicoll. Reprint. Grand Rapids: Eerdmans, 1980, II, 259, 407.

Michaelis, Wilhelm. "ὁράω εἶδον." *Theological Dictionary of the New Testament*, ed. Gerhard Friedrich; trans. and ed., G. W. Bromley, 1981, V, 316.

Piper, O. A. "Knowledge ." *The Interpreter's Dictionary of the Bible*. New York: Abingdon Press, 1962, III, 43-4.

Sanday, W. and A. C. Headlam. "The Epistle to the Romans." *The International Critical Commentary*, eds. C. A. Briggs, S. R. Driver and A. Plummer. New York: Charles Scribner's Sons, 1904, 44.

Schmitz, E. D. "Knowledge, Experience, Ignorance." *The New International Dictionary of New Testament Theology*, ed. Colin Brown. Grand Rapids: Zondervan, 1975, II, 392.

Seeseman, H. "οἶδα." *Theological Dictionary of the New Testament*, ed. Gerhard Friedrich; trans. and ed. G. W. Bromley. Grand Rapids: Eerdmans, 1981, V, 116.

2. Articles in Periodicals

Davies, W. D. "Knowledge in the Dead Sea Scrolls and Matthew 11:25-30." *Harvard Theological Review*, XLVI (July, 1953), 119-28.

Erickson, Richard J. "Oida and Ginosko and Verbal Aspect in Pauline Usage." *Westminster Theological Journal*, XLIV (1982).

Johnson, S. Lewis. "Paul and the Knowledge of God." *Bibliothecasacra*, 129 (January-March, 1972), 73-4.

Nock, A. D. "Gnosticism." *Harvard Theological Review*, 57 (October, 1964), 274.
    Picirelli, Robert E. "The Meaning of Epignosis." *The Evangelical
    Quarterly*, XLVII (1975), 87-8.

Pope, R. Martin. "Faith and Knowledge in Pauline and Johannine Thought." *The
    Expository Times*, XLI (1930), 421.

3. Essays

Burdick, Donald W. "Οἶδα and Γινώσκω in the Pauline Epistles." *New Dimen-
    sions in New Testament Study*, ed. R. N. Longenecker and M. C. Tenney.
    Grand Rapids: Zondervan, 1974, 374.

_____. "The Dead Sea Manual of Discipline." *Bulletin of the American Schools of
    Oriental Research*, trans. W. H. Brownlee. Jerusalem: American Schools of
    Oriental Research, 1951.

Quispel, G. "Gnosticism and the New Testament." *The Bible in Modern Scholar-
    ship*, ed. J. Philip Hyatt. Nashville: Abingdon Press, 1965, 265.

Silva, Moises. "The Pauline Style as Lexical Choice: ΓΙΝΏΣΚΕΙΝ and Related
    Verbs." *Pauline Studies*, ed. D. A. Hagner and M. J. Harris. Exeter: The
    Paternoster Press LTD, 1980, 197-8.

Taylor, Willard H. "The Knowledge of God." *God, Man, and Salvation*. Kansas City:
    Beacon Hill, 1977, 207-25.

4. Books

Abbott-Smith, G. *A Manual Greek Lexicon of the New Testament*. New York:
    Charles Scribner's Sons, 1936.

Albright, W. F. *New Horizons in Biblical Research*. London: Oxford University
    Press, 1966.

Allen, Tom. *A Closer Look at Dr. Laura*. Camp Hill, PA: Horizon
    Books, 1998.

Angus, S. *The Mystery Religions*. Reprint. New York: Dover Publications, Inc., 1975.

Arndt, W. F. and F. W. Gingrich. *A Greek-English Lexicon of the New Testament and Other Early Christian Literature*. Chicago: The University and Chicago Press, 1957.

Arnott, Peter D. *An Introduction to the Greek World*. London: Macmillan, 1967.

Barclay, William. *The Letters of James and Peter*. Philadelphia: The Westminster Press, 1960.

_____. *The Letters of John and Jude*. Philadelphia: The Westminster Press, 1960.

Barrett, C. K. *A Commentary on the Epistle to the Romans*. New York: Harper & Row, 1957.

Beet, J. A. *A Commentary on St. Paul's Epistle to the Romans*. Reprint. Salem, OH: Allegheny Publications, 1982.

Bevan, Edwyn. *Hellenism and Christianity*. Reprint. Freeport: Books for Libraries Press, Inc., 1967.

The Bible, King James Version

The Bible, New King James Version

The Bible, New International Version

Bousset, Wilhelm. *Kyrios Christos*, trans. John E. Steely. Nashville: Abingdon Press, 1970.

Bowra. *The Greek Experience*. Cleveland: The World Publishing Co., 1957.

Bultmann, Rudolf. *The Gospel of John a Commentary*, trans. G. R. Beasley-Murray, R. W. N. Hoare and J. K. Riches. Philadelphia: The Westminster Press, 1971.

_____. *Theology of the New Testament*, I, trans. Kendrick Grobel. New York: Charles Scribner's & Sons, 1951.

Clarke, Adam. *Clarke's Commentary*. Nashville: Abingdon, I.

Corwin, Virginia. *St. Ignatius and Christianity in Antioch*. New Haven: Yale University Press, 1960.

Cottrell, Jack. *The Faith Once for All: Bible Doctrine for Today*. Jolin, MO: College Press Publishing Co., 2002.

Danielou, Jean. *The Theology of Jewish Christianity*, trans. and ed. John A. Baker. Chicago: The Henry Regnery Company, 1964.

Dodd, C. H. *The Bible and the Greeks*. London: Hodder and Stoughton, 1954.

_____. *The Interpretation of the Fourth Gospel*. London: The Cambridge University Press, 1958.

Earp, R. F. *The Way of the Greeks*. London: Oxford University Press, 1929.

Finley, M. I. *The Ancient Greeks*. New York: The Viking Press, 1965.

Foerster, Werner. *Gnosis*, English translation edited by R. McL. Wilson. London: Oxford University Press, 1972.

Glover, T. R. *The World of the New Testament*. New York: Macmillan, 1931.

Godbey, W. B. *Commentary on the New Testament*. Cincinnati: Revivalist Office, 1899, V.

Godwin, Joscelyn. *Mystery Religions in the Ancient World*. San Francisco: Harper & Row, 1981.

Grant, Robert M. *Gnosticism*. Reprint. New York : AMS Press, 1978.

Guthrie, Donald. *New Testament Introduction—Hebrews to Revelation*. Chicago: Inter-Varsity Press, 1966.

Grant, R. M. *Gnosticism and Early Christianity*. New York: Columbia University Press, 1959.

Hamilton, Edith. *The Greek Way*. Reprint. New York: W. W. Norton, 1964.

Hatch, Edwin and Henry A. Redpath. *A Concordance to the Septuagint*. Graz-Austria: Akademische Druck-U. Verlagsanstaldt, 1954, I.

Hooper, Finley. *Greek Realities.* London: Rupert Hart-Davis LTD, 1968.

Jaeger, Werner. *Paideia: The Ideals of Greek Culture,* trans. Gilbert Highet. New York: Oxford University Press, 1945, I, II, III.

Jonas, Hans. *The Gnostic Religion.* Boston: Beacon Press, 1958.

Lacarriere, Jacques. *The Gnostics.* New York: E. P. Dutton, 1977.

Liddell, Henry George and Robert Scott. *A Greek-English Lexicon.* Oxford: University Press, 1953.

Lightfoot, J. B. *Notes on the Epistles of St. Paul.* Reprint. Winona Lake: Alpha Publications, 1979.

_____. *St. Paul's Epistles to the Colossians and to Philemon.* Reprint. Grand Rapids: Zondervan, 1965.

_____. *St. Paul's Epistles to the Galatians.* Reprint. London: Macmillan, 1921.

_____. *Saint Paul's Epistle to the Philippians.* Grand Rapids: Zondervan, 1965.

Luther, Martin. *A Commentary on St. Paul's Epistle to the Galatians,* trans. Theodore Graebner. Grand Rapids: Zondervan, n.d.

MacGregor, Geddes. *Gnosis.* Wheaton: The Theosophical Publishing House, 1979.

Machen, J. Gresham. *New Testament Greek for Beginners.* New York: Macmillan, 1965.

_____. *The Origin of Paul's Religion.* Reprint. Grand Rapids: Eerdmans, 1978.

McDowell. *Evidence That Demands a Verdict.* San Bernardino: Campus Crusade for Christ, 1972.

Meyer, H. A. W. *Critical and Exegetical Handbook to the Epistles to the Philippians and Colossians.* Reprint. Peabody: Hendrickson Publishers, Inc., 1983.

_____. *The Epistle to the Romans,* trans. J. C. Moore, E. Johnson, and W. P. Dickson. Reprint. Peabody: Hendrickson, 1983.

Morgan, G. Campbell. *The Acts of the Apostles.* Tappan: Revell, 1924.

Morris, Leon. *The First Epistle of Paul to the Corinthians.* Grand Rapids: Eerdmans, 1980.

_____. *The Gospel According to John.* Grand Rapids: Eerdmans, 1971.

Moulton, James Hope and James Milligan. *The Vocabulary of the Greek Testament.* Grand Rapids: Eerdmans, 1963.

Moulton, W. F. and A. S. Geden. *A Concordance to the Greek Testament.* Edinburgh: T. & T. Clark, 1950.

Murray, Gilbert. *Five Stages of Greek Religion.* Reprint. New York: AMS Press, 1978.

Nash, Donald A. *New Testament Word Studies.* Grayson: Witness Press, 1982.

Neill, Stephen. *The Interpretation of the New Testament.* London: Oxford University Press, 1964.

Newman, A. H. *A Manual of Church History.* Valley Forge: Judson Press, 1964, I.

Northrop, F. S. C. *The Meeting of East and West.* New York: Macmillan, 1946.

Packer, J. I. *Knowing God.* Downer's Grove, IL: InterVarsity Press, 1973.

Purkiser, W. T., R. S. Taylor, and W. H. Taylor. *God, Man, and Salvation.* Kansas City: Beacon Hill Press, 1977.

Ramm, Bernard. *The Witness of the Spirit.* Grand Rapids: Eerdmans, 1960.

Reitzenstein, Richard. *Hellenistic Mystery-Religions,* trans. John. E. Steely. Pittsburgh: The Pickwick Press, 1978.

Richardson, Alan. *An Introduction to the Theology of the New Testament.* New York: Harper & Row, 1958.

Robinson, J. Armitage. *St. Paul's Epistle to the Ephesians.* London: Macmillan, 1909.

Schmithals, Walter. *Gnosticism in Corinth,* trans. John E. Steely. Nashville: Abingdon, 1971.

Simcox, William Henry. *The Writers of the New Testament.* Winona Lake: Alpha Publications, 1980.

Stifler, James M. *The Epistle to the Romans.* Chicago: Moody, 1960.

Strong, James. *The Exhaustive Concordance of the Bible.* New York: Abingdon, 1961.

Thayer, J. H. *A Greek-English Lexicon of the New Testament.* Grand Rapids: Baker Book House, 1980.

Turner, Nigel. *Grammatical Insights into the New Testament.* Edinburgh: T. & T. Clark, 1977.

Vine, W. E. *An Expository Dictionary of New Testament Words.* Westwood: Revell, 1961.

Wesley, John. *Explanatory Notes upon the New Testament.* Reprint. Salem, OH: Schmul, 1976.

_____. *Works.* Reprint. Grand Rapids: Baker, V, VI, 1978.

Westcott, B. F. *The Epistles of St. John.* Reprint. Grand Rapids: Wm. B. Eerdmans Publishing Co., 1982.

_____. *Some Lessons of the Revised Version of the New Testament.* New York: James Pott and Co., 1897.

Whedon, D. D. *Commentary on the New Testament.* Reprint. Salem, OH: Schmul, VI, 1977.

Wiley, H. Orton. *Christian Theology.* Kansas City: Beacon Hill, I, 1960.

Wilson, R. McL. *The Gnostic Problem.* London: A. R. Mowbray & Co. LTD, 1979.

Yamauchi, Edwin. *Pre-Christian Gnosticism.* Grand Rapids: Eerdmans, 1973.